10 Step KPI System

A time-proven approach to finding tailor-made
KPIs for the most challenging business situations

10 Step KPI System

A time-proven approach to finding tailor-made KPIs
for the most challenging business situations

Aleksey Savkin

Aleksey Savkin
2017

BSC Designer

First Printing: 2017

ISBN 978-1-365-90071-6

To my parents and spouse for their immeasurable support

Contents

Introduction

How this book is different from 796 other titles on Amazon

The term "KPI" has become a buzzword. Experts suggest the best KPIs for certain business applications, as well as discuss the checklists, and must-have metrics that need to exist in any business. I searched in the books section on Amazon for the "KPI" keyword and got 796 results. How is my book different? It is not another review of theory, it is a step-by-step guide with proven techniques, the KPI System.

My promise for the book

Before writing a single sentence, I formulated my promises to the readers and to myself about what I want this book to be like in the end. These principles helped me many times to stay on the right track with my writing. Here they are:

- **Create a practical guide.** If one of the users of BSC Designer asks "How to find a good KPI for ..." – I want this book to provide a perfect answer
- **Step-by-step system.** I want to share in this book the best practices that proven to work, a tested system, not just a list of disconnected recommendations
- **Challenge readers.** I'll challenge my readers with the questions and experiments. Instead of following standard receipts, I want you to be able to make your own ones.

- **Be visual.** To compete with other business books on your bookshelf, I'll use such tools as interesting stories, well-structured content, and nice illustrations.

- **Keep it short.** There are certain page number standards for a good business book, but having in mind the first and the second principles, my last promise was to keep the book short and informative.

How the KPI System was created

My interest in the domain of the performance measurement started when I was working on my thesis project at MEPhI (Moscow Engineering Physics Institute). My supervising professor suggested focusing the research on such emerging topics as the "Balanced Scorecard." It was not something typical for a student from the Cybernetics faculty, and was probably more applicable to the MBA program, but the fusion between the scorecard math and building business models looked very attractive to me. In a few weeks, I created the first prototype of the software for the scorecards and KPIs, and it was called Strategy2Act. That project was a great way to engage with that problem area, get my first feedbacks, and understand more the needs of the end users. Later, I was engaged in some other software projects as founder and co-founder. Those experiments helped me to get a sense of the business side of the software industry. With the help of a new team, I decided to get back to the idea of business scorecards, and in 2004 the completely new software called BSC Designer was released.

From the very beginning at BSC Designer we wanted not just to give users an automation tool for the scorecards, but to support their efforts from the conceptual perspective. I was interested in learning the best practices myself, and sharing them with the users. Working with different types of clients, we gave an opportunity to work with different types of scorecards. Some were excellent management tools and were a source of inspiration, some were overloaded with less useful metrics, and helped to understand typical problems and formulate the recommendations to avoid. At that stage, there was no formal system for KPIs, all the advice about metrics were tailor made for each customer and each specific case.

In contrast to the classical consultants who build a scorecard and forget about their clients next month, we were trying to be helpful in the long term. BSC Designer experts, including me, were writing articles about performance measurement and strategy execution, and analyzing different aspects of those problems areas. We also created and shared publicly some examples of the strategy and KPIs scorecards. It's a great feeling when someone gets in touch with you on LinkedIn just to tell you that your articles were useful and are now a reference in some research papers.

The first formal version of the KPI System appeared in 2014. It included 10 steps and a nice-looking one-page diagram that helped teams to brainstorm difficult cases. The next version included 12 steps: the additional steps were an explicit formulation of the breakdown, stakeholders, and business context steps, but very soon it appeared that the three separate steps looked nice on paper, but in practical use they did not make any sense. In the current KPI System you will find Step 1 with an introduction to these three concepts, all the supporting ideas are illustrated by the examples. I found that this form works much better for the readers.

In the first two versions, there was a *Step 7 – Execution* that looked very important, but the real use of the system showed that most of the users already had a good execution plan in mind on the very first step. At the same time, the biggest struggles were with finding leading indicators, so I decided to replace the "Execution" step with a few framing ideas about finding leading indicators.

Is it the final version? I hope no! I'm interested in learning how you use the System and to improve it even more!

Executive summary

This is a 3-page executive summary of the book. Use it to quickly learn about the problems discussed in the book and the suggested solutions. For more details review the steps of the KPIs System.

How to find indicators

- Agree about the subject, stakeholders and the purpose of measurement
    - If we can achieve this agreement, then we can quantify and measure
    - Intangibles like "value" and "performance" need to be broken-down into smaller tangible parts first
- The value of measurement is not just in finding the numbers, but in reaching an agreement about the goals and their meaning
    - The best KPIs are the product of the discussion
    - Skipping the discussion phase leads to problems with motivation
- Analyze your system to find the points of measurement:
    - Constraints of the system are the first candidate for the indicators
    - Look at the success factors, and expected outcomes; learn to differentiate them from the inputs and activities

- o The best indicators are aligned with the strategic (change) goals
- o Make sure you have indicators for value, quality, performance, customers, and conversion rates
- o Apply silver metric test to find the most important indicator
- For the areas of unknown:
  - o Prepare experiments
  - o Observe what your clients do
  - o Put yourself in client's shoes

How to build a scorecard

- Do a technical setup for your metrics: define scale, weight, performance formulas, and benchmarks
- Keep your measurement efforts focused
  - o Reduce costs by making your systems measurable by design
  - o Promote culture of performance measurement
- Use decision matrix to sort your indicators into operational, strategic, ones that you can outsource, and ones that you don't need

How to implement scorecard and KPIs

- Once the new measurement system is introduced, plan to control the induced behavior: use a pair of performance and quality indicators

- Detect and avoid typical mistakes:
  - Metrics without context; goals without metrics; only "good news" indicators
  - Mix of goal, indicator, and action plan
  - Make sure that your metrics allow you to learn from both: success and failure

- Cascade your strategy:
  - The KPIs should support the strategy discussion on all levels
  - Cascade your strategy by business goals, not by KPIs
  - Find appropriate indicators for cascaded goals

- Your job is not to maintain an Excel spreadsheet with KPIs or strategy maps in PowerPoint - use automation tools to save your time

From observation and quantification to the metrics and KPIs

"We had a long list of the KPIs, but it was not really useful for us... People were chasing for the specific KPIs, the performance was good, but our company was finally losing money."

A CEO about scorecard system

Before discussing the steps of the KPI System it makes sense to introduce some basics of the measurement domain. One of the terms that we often hear in this context is "quantification." The verb "to quantify" it is often used interchangeably with the verb "to measure." Other terms like "metric," "indicator" and "KPI" are also often used as synonyms. In the business world, there is no agreement about these terms. And if you want to start working on improving your performance measurement system, it is good idea to achieve that agreement, at least in your organization.

In this chapter, I'm using two examples to introduce the terms and illustrate the difference between them. I'm sharing the explanation of the terms that I feel comfortable about and that have been proven to work for our customers.

An example of the metric: the cost to gain a new customer

Let's start with an example of a simple metric. One of the most important indicators in your business is the cost to gain a new customer. By the way, do you know what that cost is for your business? If not, it is easy to calculate it! Measure the number of the new customers you had in, let's say, last 12 months; find out the total costs for marketing over those 12 months. Then divide marketing costs by the number of the customers. What do we have in the result? A **metric** – "cost to gain a new customer!"

An example of the observation and quantification: measuring happiness

What about more complex cases, when for example, we are talking about "happiness?" One can say that happiness is not tangible and it's not possible to measure it, but The United Nations organization would not agree, and they even rank countries by their happiness level in the World Happiness Report.

What's the trick? How do they know that people in Germany are happier than people in Spain[1]? The answer is simple: instead of measuring intangible "happiness," they **observed** people living in different countries, defined certain evaluation criteria, and **quantified** them using data that is relatively easy to collect. The result is a ranking table in the World Happiness Report.

Someone might argue: what's the benefit of measuring happiness in this way, or measuring happiness at all in the business environment? I

---

[1]Per the World Happiness Report 2017 ranking Germany is on 16th place and Spain is on 34th

would respond that everything depends on your context. For example, Tony Hsieh, CEO at Zappos in his book "Delivering happiness"[2] argued that focusing on customer's and employee's happiness can be a company's long-term strategy. And it seems to have worked for Zappos so far.

Another example might be Southwest Airlines that puts employee happiness above customer satisfaction[3]. How does the employee happiness metric look for you now? Probably in your case it might work as a shortcut towards increasing a value for customers...

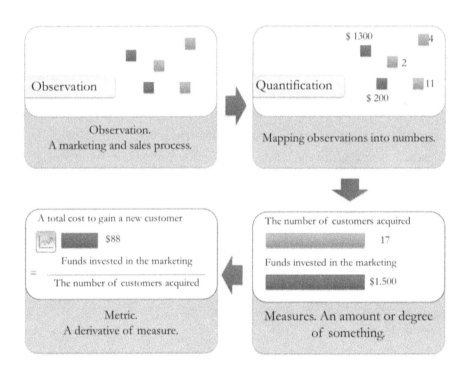

Figure 1 From observation and quantification to the metrics and KPIs

[2]Delivering Happiness. A path to profits, passion, and purpose, Tony Hsieh, Business Plus, 2010. Book's website.

[3]Southwest   Airlines   "Gets   It"   With   Our   Culture," https://www.southwestaircommunity.com/t5/Southwest-Stories/Southwest-Airlines-Gets-It-With-Our-Culture/ba-p/36414

3 Steps: Observation, Quantification, Metrics

In these two examples, we can see the 3 steps of the measurement process: observation, quantification and getting measures, getting metrics - the derivatives from measures. What about the first example, "The cost to gain a new customer?" Where are the "observation" and "quantification" steps there? Let's do it again, for the purpose of clarifying the steps and their meaning.

Observation

If we have an abstract look at the business model of most for-profit businesses, we could see that the company is somehow getting new clients. We can learn that this happens because of the existing marketing and sales systems. And we might suppose that there are certain costs to run both systems. The output of the sales system are the new paying customers.

Quantification

We are curious, and we want to get a sense of how exactly this business is working. On this step, we start *quantifying*. According to Wikipedia[4], quantification is about mapping human observations into numbers. In our case, we can quantify the input of marketing activities as the quantity of money invested, and the output of the sales system as the quantity of the new clients generated.

---

[4]"Quantification is the act of counting and measuring that maps human sense observations and experiences into quantities." https://en.wikipedia.org/wiki/Quantification_(science)

Measures

As defined in Merriam-Webster dictionary a measure is "an amount or degree of something." In our example, we can have two measures: "The number of customers acquired" and "Funds invested into the marketing, $."

Metrics

Now, what is a *metric*? One of the definitions in Merriam-Webster dictionary is that "a metric is a standard of measurement." The definition looks very similar to the definition of the term *"measure."* In fact, in the business world the terms "metric" and "measure" overlap in meaning. One explanation that I find useful is that metric is a *derivative* of measure. In our example, we can say that the derivative of the two metrics "The number of customers acquired" and "Funds invested into the marketing" is a "A total cost to gain a new customer, $" metric.

KPI term

KPI is an acronym for the Key Performance Indicator.

Why it is "key" indicator

By definition, any indicator has a certain connection to how a business is performing. First of all, we are interested in focusing on those indicators that have high importance in the context of the business strategy of an organization. It also means that an indicator that is "key" for one organization, might be a simple metric for another.

Why it is a "performance" indicator

The best choice for the term "performance" in the Merriam Webster dictionary is "the fulfillment of a claim, promise, or request." We are talking about business performance, so it can be defined as the fulfillment of a claim that a company does in their strategy, or promises to the stakeholders.

What is an indicator?

Before we discussed how the term *"metric"* is defined. To keep things simple, let's agree that *indicator* is its synonym. For sure, dictionaries define these terms differently, but I think that for the context of the performance measurement the difference is insignificant.

What is a metric? Formally, the term was defined above, but in simple words it is a **number**! For example, "How good our customers are engaged" is not really a metric as it did not pass the "quantification" step and it's hard to say what numerical value should we use for the engagement. In contrast, "Average customer engagement score, according to the monthly survey" is an indicator. We know that it is a number, and we even know how to get the value for it.

Why the term KPI is bad?

The worst thing about the term "KPI is that it's used too often as a synonym for a simple metric. All KPIs are metrics, but most of the metrics are not KPIs. For example, "the cost to get a new customer" is a good KPI for most business contexts, but another indicator - "the number of computers per employee" is a simple metric. If you want to stay on safe ground then use the term "metric," instead of "KPI."

Test: KPI vs. Simple Metric

If you are not sure if you are dealing with a KPI or a simple metric, do a simple test: imagine that you can double the value of this indicator. If you expect the performance of the business to be increased significantly, then it's a good KPI for your business context, if not, then it is a simple metric. The metric from the previous example - "The number of computers in an office per an employee" - is not really connected to the ultimate business performance. If you will double the number of computers, you don't expect your profits to be increased significantly.

Why the term KPI is good?

With all the disadvantages of the term "KPI" there are two benefits that make it useful: it is well known in business world, and it is just 3 symbols long. We often hear people say: "We need some good KPIs for this!" While the term KPI might be confusing, still everyone understands that it is about quantifying and measuring things. And it is just 3 characters long. For examples, in BSC Designer software we have a "KPI" tab. Among all the options: "KPI," "indicator," "metric," or "measure," it's the shortest one. Moreover, in many languages the translation of this term is not needed.

Goals and objectives

These are synonyms again. Some authors, including me, define *goals* as something broad, intangible, or abstract, and *objectives* as something more specific, tangible, and measurable. For me, the objective sounds a lot like a combination of a goal, metric, target, and action plan. Below I explain why this mix is dangerous for the performance measurement system, that's why when I can choose between these two terms, I prefer "goal."

Mixing terms

Following S.M.A.R.T.[5] criteria acronym many business professionals are trying to make their goals comply with it. How do you like a *goal* formulated in this way: "Increase revenue by 10% within a 1 year period by attracting clients from new geographies?" It looks smart on the annual strategic plans, but how is one supposed to use it in practice? Here are just a few potential problems:

- If the company increased revenues by other means as well, should it be counted in this 10% planned increase?
- If teams have other ideas to increase revenue, not just from "new geographies," should they add a new "goal" like this one?
- It says we need to improve in 1 year, but what measure should one use for monthly reports?

---

[5] SMART acronym stands for Specific, Measurable, Achievable, Relevant, Time-bound

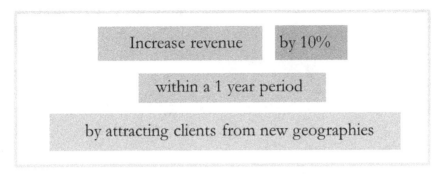

Figure 2 Avoid mixing goals, metrics, targets, and action plans

A better approach would be to break down this phrase into separate parts:

- **Goal**: Increase revenue
- **Metric**: Revenue growth, %
- **Target**: 10% within 1 year
- **Action plan**: attract clients from new geographies

We talk more about formal definition of metrics in Step 5 of the KPI System.

Agree on the terms

To avoid the confusion, be sure to spend time on the definition of the terms, at least at the level of your organization or business unit. Some organizations have long traditions of using certain vocabulary for the performance measurement domain. There is no need to replace it with a new one, just make sure that everyone is on the same page.

Why should one measure business performance?

> "Now the general who wins a battle makes many calculations in his head ere the battle is fought. The general who loses a battle makes but a few calculations beforehand. Thus do many calculations lead to victory, and a few calculations to defeat: how much more for no calculation at all! It is by attention to this point that I can foresee who is likely to win or lose."
>
> *Sun Tzu, The Art of War*

Why should one measure a business performance? A quick answer is that you can run your business without measurement, metrics, KPIs, etc., but as Chinese military strategist Sun Tzu said, you can improve your chances to win, if you do calculations beforehand.

Perception and contextual biases

Human beings are not that good in measurement. If you need a quick way to convince those who are skeptical about the need of measurement in your company, use visual illustrations as a fun and engaging example. On my workshops, I like using the simple yet effective variation of Müller-Lyer illusion. Here is a simple task: have a look at the picture below and tell me which line is shorter?

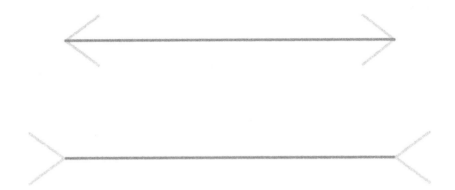

Figure 3 Which line is shorter? A variation of Müller-Lyer illusion

As you might have already guessed the length of the black lines is the same. Just draw some straight vertical lines to confirm this. This quick demonstration is not only about the perception bias; it's also an example of the contextual bias. By asking to find a *shorter* line I set a context for you that the lines are different in length. What would be the result if I would ask you to find out if those lines are the same in length or not? By the way, in my question I did not mention that you had to choose between black lines. It seemed like this requirement is implied, but it was not; you could pick any green line as an answer.

What gets measured gets improved. Doesn't it?

There is a known saying: "What gets measured gets improved." Is it correct? It depends! For example, if we want to win a game, we certainly need to know the score. If we invest some effort in measurement, then we can expect a better understanding of the subject of measurement, and then achieve better results. Finally, with a good measurement in place, we will have some strong feedback data that will help us to improve.

The problem is that some managers follow the "what gets measured gets improved" mantra literally. Instead of discussing the subject of measurement in the details, and focusing their measurement efforts on what is important, they mainly focus on measures themselves. They invert in and actively promote a new mantra: "More measures - better results." This approach does more harm than good. The performance scorecards of such managers are overloaded with the metrics, and it's hard to get any business insight from the data.

Accountability and reporting

When we talk to the customers of BSC Designer about the KPIs, in many cases they explain, that the metrics that they are looking for will help to improve **accountability** in their organization and give a common framework for the **reporting**.

Sounds smart, right? I normally prefer to ask a few more questions about what exactly is meant by the "accountability" and "reporting." As the results depend a lot on how exactly the performance measurement and management systems are implemented.

Positive scenario: metric in the red zone help to focus the discussion

Imagine a scenario when there is some good marketing metric like "Leads to sales conversion rate, %" with "5% increase" target for the next month. What should happen at the end of the month if that target will **not** be achieved?

First, it should be noted in the performance reports. Second, the team should start a discussion about the reasons for the current results and revise their action plan if needed. This approach gives a positive feedback loop to the persons responsible for the metric.

Negative scenario: carrot and stick management style

Another approach to the accountability is when indicators are linked to some incentives: "Keep indicators is in the green zone and you will have your incentive; if an indicator gets in the red zone –you will not have your incentive."

If that's what "**accountability**" means in your organization, then you are at risk. You might not just demotivate your team, but you could also induce an undesired behavior. For more details check out the "Reward scorecard" in the "Examples" section.

Metrics help to define vague goals

Any organization has a goal: "Improve the quality of the service to the customers." Let's use it as an example. How do we quantify and measure the *quality* of the service? We can survey our clients and get a "customer service satisfaction rate, %." This is a lagging indicator, similar to a rear-view mirror in your car, it tells a good story, but about something that has already happened.

If we want to improve, we need to find some root-cause connections between what the organization does and how this influences the customer service quality. In other words, we need to understand what "high quality customer service" means for the clients. We need to break down a vague idea of "high-quality customer service" into more tangible parts. For example, parts could be "Waiting time," "Service time," and "First contact resolution rate."

Now we can align these metrics with the goal "Improve the quality of the service to the customers." Instead of dealing with a vague idea of "quality" we can now work with more specific goals like decreasing waiting time, and increasing first contact resolution rate. To learn more about this approach check out Step 1 and Step 7 of the KPI System.

Metrics are motivating

In the "My promise for the book" chapter I shared the principles that I formulated before writing this book. The last promise was to keep it short and informative, and I needed some benchmarks to fulfil this promise. I looked at my bookshelf, picked my favorite business book, and did some basic calculations to find out the number of words in it. That will be my quantity benchmark.

Having this target in mind, I divided the number of words by 30 days to get a daily goal. Why 30? Just for motivation! A short research showed that some good books were written even in a shorter period. Then I created a basic dashboard with a daily target and overall progress calculation. Will it help to write a better book? Probably not, but it reminded me daily that it's time to work on the book. Simple and effective motivational tool.

But there are businesses that don't measure their performance...

If you don't have a nice-looking dashboard, it doesn't mean that you don't have a measurement system. Take the owners of a one-man business as an example, they normally won't have a shiny real-time dashboard on their smartphones, but ask those entrepreneurs about their profits or running costs, and you can be sure they will have a number.

What if the questions are more difficult? For example: "What's the cost to get a new lead?" "What's the conversion rate from the leads to the sales?" "How does this data depend on the geo profile of the client?" "How did the conversion change after we implemented a new CRM?" It will be hard to answer these questions without having a more formal set of metrics. As always, there are many exceptions and nuances, and we will talk about them below in the KPI System.

There is something that we cannot measure

> "All qualities can be expressed quantitatively, 'qualitative' does not mean unmeasurable."
>
> *The Principle Of 'Quality Quantification,' Tom Gilb*

Can we quantify and measure anything? If we can agree on the subject of the measurement and on the context, then we can. In the steps of the KPI System I will share specific recommendations about how to deal with challenging measurement situations. Consider this chapter as a motivational one.

Measuring employee engagement

Let's talk about another example – "employee engagement." Intuitively we understand that higher employee engagement is better. Someone can probably do an employee survey in their company to find out an engagement index. From the first look "employee engagement" looks like something intangible, hard to quantify and measure. But it is not.

According to Gallup[6], employee engagement is one of the factors that is strongly related to the organizational outcomes. Just some data:

---

[6] How Employee Engagement Drives Growth, Susan Sorenson, 2013, Gallup http://www.gallup.com/businessjournal/163130/employee-engagement-drives-growth.aspx

25% of business units with the highest employee engagement (compared to the rest of the units with lower employee engagement), showed:

- 22% higher profitability
- 65% lower turnover (in low-turnover organizations)
- 48% fewer safety incidents

Moreover, in the Gallup Q12® Meta-Analysis Report one can find specific factors that can lead to an increase in employee engagement. I certainly do recommend checking out this report. What is more important is that it works as a "proof of concept" that even something intangible like engagement level can be broken down into quantifiable and actionable parts. Of course this works only if you and your team agree with the viewpoint of Gallup´s specialists on the employee engagement.

Measuring Happiness

When we were discussing the difference between quantification and measurement, I mentioned the UN World Happiness Report. They quantified something personal and intangible like feeling of happiness using such factors as:

- Social support
- Health life expectancy
- Freedom to make life choices, and others

Did they have some numbers? Sure! Are those numbers useful? Yes! In some context, for some applications, they are. Are they the main or the only factors of the happiness? Probably not. One of the conclusions from that example is that we can quantify and measure anything, but before doing so we must agree on certain assumptions, like what is the subject of measurement, who is involved, what's the purpose of measurement and how the results will be used. These assumptions are important. We discuss them in Step 1 of the KPI System, so, don't skip this step even if it looks like an obvious one.

Measuring employee's mood

What about an employee's mood? It looks like it is even less tangible than engagement, but still, we can find some simple approach to quantifying it. Look at the example of Barcelona-based Celpax. They produce a simple device that one can put on the office wall next to the entrance door. The interface of the device gives a possibility of answering a single question: "How was your day?"

The scale for the answer doesn't require any further explanation. There is a green zone marked by a positive smile and the red zone marked by a frown. Then the software calculates "Mood KPI" and displays it on the online dashboard using a 0 – 100% scale. Do these "mood" numbers make any sense? I believe the use of absolute numbers is limited, but one can find a lot of insights if you are looking at how the data changed over time, and comparing it to what was happening in the organization. Once again, the best method for measurement depends on how we are going to use the data.

An exception that proves the rule

In the "Examples" chapter I shared a case of measurement of the leadership training effectiveness. When discussing this case with our client we were not able to achieve an agreement about what leadership is. How can we say that someone is a good leader? We started discussing the historical personalities, and even in those cases, the opinions were always contradictory. We could not agree on the subject of measurement; thus, we could not go ahead with the quantification. That is a case that just proves the rule.

Typical problems with KPIs

At BSC Designer we regularly do our own surveys to find out what the typical challenges are about KPIs and scorecards that business professionals face. The data varies from year to year, but the top 3 are always the same: finding good metrics and KPIs; motivation to use KPIs and the challenge of misuse; overload with KPIs. In this chapter, we will discuss these problems, as well as possible ways to avoid them.

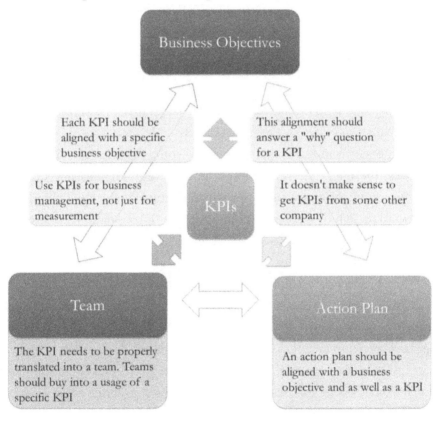

Figure 4 Why most KPIs don't work and what to do about this

Misalignment between goals, KPIs, and employees

In one of previous articles I mentioned **misalignment** as the main problem in the KPIs world. KPIs exist, teams spend time on maintaining scorecards, but for some reason they are not working as expected. Have a look at the diagram below. That's a simple picture of what we want to achieve – a coherence between goals, teams, and action using KPI as our ally. The KPI needs to be properly translated into a team. Teams should buy into a usage of a specific KPI.

Finding good metrics and KPIs

How does a "bad" KPIs appear on a dashboard? A typical case is when a boss follows the "what gets measured, gets done" mantra and asks someone from the company to find "some good KPIs." As it often happens. the quest for KPIs starts on the search engines like Google, and very soon a long list of the metrics is compiled into the PowerPoint presentation. The presented KPIs normally look smart, but there is always a strange feeling like those are not exactly what the company needs to focus on right now.

The KPI report then lives its bureaucratic life and in the best case is used once a year to show that there was some progress. During such annual reviews, many of the reported KPIs show nothing but some random performance changes, and after some discussions a logical conclusion comes up: there is a problem with KPIs, they are wrong and don't work for our business. Let's now find some better ones! If that's your case, go ahead with the steps of the KPI System!

Motivation to use KPIs and misuse problem

Teams with more disciplined management are not as lucky as those teams where the use of "bad" KPIs is limited by reporting purposes only. If management insists on daily use of the "bad" KPIs, they soon find out that there are two problems:

1. Their employees are not enthusiastic about KPIs as much as management is
2. Sooner or later the employees find a way to game the system, e.g. keep KPIs in a green zone without achieving what was expected.

We will talk more about the gaming of measurement system in Step 8 of the KPI System.

Overload with KPIs

That's probably one of the harmless problems with the KPIs. The list of the metrics grows without any system, and soon maintaining an Excel Spreadsheet with KPIs starts taking too much valuable time from the business professionals. The solution in this case is to clean up the list of metrics by prioritizing what's important, removing what's not relevant, and outsourcing what can be outsourced. We will talk more about specific techniques for prioritization of KPIs in Step 6 of the KPI System.

What about automation? Will it help to manage the situation of KPIs overload? I see this often – someone starts using BSC Designer software and it certainly works much better for the KPIs than a standard spreadsheet software, but the trick is not about choosing the right software for automation, it's about building a clear performance measurement system first, and then automating it with the software tools.

Measurement culture

In the situations described above we faced with a certain behavior patterns related to the performance measurement. In the steps of the KPI System we discuss a lot of the ideas that might help in this case, but any efforts will be useless if the underlying culture is not ready. On Step 9 of the KPI System I talk about culture, and give some specific instructions to building a good one.

10 Step System for the Most Challenging KPIs

"Building a boat isn't about weaving canvas, forging nails, or reading the sky. It's about giving a shared taste for the sea…"

Citadelle, Antoine de Saint-Exupéry

In one of the previous chapters I shared some pragmatic reasons about why an organization should use KPIs. But probably the most important reason was not mentioned: the breakthroughs that happen when a team discusses new metrics. If you have the resources to implement only a single idea from this book, take this one: "Think that KPIs are the process, not just the result."

In other words, make sure that all of the metrics that you have on your dashboards and scorecards, are the product of the discussion, and that the insights generated during those discussions are methodically written down. The steps of the KPI System will help you to guide and focus such discussions. Sometimes you will have a temptation to stop the "useless" talks and mandate metrics that you think are right. Don't do this, instead try to communicate your ideas in the style of Socratic dialogs.

How to use the KPI System

Here are some general recommendations about using the system:

- First, review quickly all of the steps and get an idea about the suggested approach in general
- Check out the "Examples" section, probably there is something that will capture your attention in the first place
- In the "Downloads" section of the book there is a print-friendly version of the KPI System template. Download it and print your copy.
- Go ahead with the steps of the KPI System. Fill in the KPI Template to make your reading experience more interactive.
- Use the ideas from Step 2 to review the KPIs that already exist in your company
- Ask your colleagues to be your opponents when reading Step 8, discuss with them the behavior that the indicators might induce.
- After trying the steps of the KPI System yourself, try to explain them to your colleagues
- When you have practiced enough with the System, read the "Build a scorecard" chapter and try communicating your strategy across the company
- Share your feedback with BSC Designer team and other readers. For example, you can share it on the Amazon website where others can read your comment

Step 1. Define measurement prism

In optics, transparent prisms are used to disperse the visible light into spectral colors. A measurement prism works in a similar way – it helps to break down intangible qualitive concepts into more tangible parts. To define a measurement prism one needs to answer these three questions:

1. What is the subject of measurement?

2. Who are the stakeholders?

3. What is the purpose of measurement?

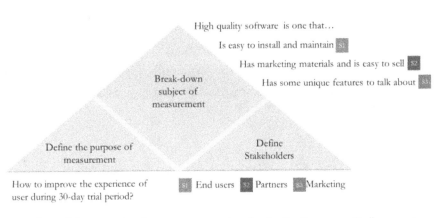

MEASUREMENT PRISM
Define subject, purpose, and stakeholders

Figure 5 An example of measurement prism for the "software quality" concept

Breaking down the subject of measurement

What is the subject of measurement? From the first look this question might look like an obvious one. Once I suggested this step to the client from the software industry and his response was something like this: "We have been in the business for 2 decades and of course we know what we want to measure! We want to measure the **quality of our software**!" That's a very good starting point, but what exactly is a "quality" applied to the domain of software products, and specifically to the client's business?

One of the definitions of quality from Merriam-Webster is "degree of excellence." But who can judge if the software has achieved a certain level of excellence or not? And talking about the term "excellence," what exactly do we mean by this? Is it excellence in the stability, user interface, functionality, and ownership cost?

And if one is looking for the excellence in stability, what exactly do we mean by "stability" in that case? Quality is many things for many people, and before we go ahead with quantification and measurement, we need to be specific about what exactly we mean by quality. The goal of this step is to break down the subject of measurement into some tangible parts. To be able to do this efficiently and effectively, we will need to know who is involved in the subject of measurement, who are the stakeholders.

Finding stakeholders

In the previous step, I mentioned that quality is many things for many people. Who is involved? End users of the software, for sure. Is there anybody else who cares about the quality? There are more people involved: software developers who will appreciate a high-quality architecture and well documented software; testers who will be able to do their job well if the software has certain interfaces that make testing easier; and customer support staff who will appreciate if the documentations for the software is clear and helpful.

The list goes on. The idea is that we need to understand who will be involved as it narrows down the variety of concepts that we have to deal with. Probably after such brainstorming you will decide to focus on the quality of documentation only, or on the quality from the viewpoint of user-critical problems.

The list of the stakeholder is not just the list of persons, but the systems as well. Here is a definition of a stakeholder by Tom Gilb: "Stakeholders are any person, group or system, that have or we want to have an interest in our project."[7] For example, if the developers of the software are going to submit it to Apple Store, then the list of the stakeholders in the context of quality will be extended by a "system" represented by the requirements of the Apple Store.

Why do we measure?

Another way to focus measurement efforts is to answer the question: what is the purpose of measurement? In other words: "How are we going to use the results obtained from the measurement?" The purpose of measurement will influence the tools and methods used for measurement. The more precise information we need, the higher is the cost to get this information, but in many cases, we don't need to have precise data.

Let's take "**perceived** software quality" as an example. Let's assume that the purpose of measurement in this case is to compare two software products and to find out which one is better, and what product is the preferred choice. We can try two approaches.

---

[7] Concept Glossary, Stakeholder, Tom Gilb, http://concepts.gilb.com/definition-Stakeholder?structure=Glossary&page_ref_id=204

First approach is to do a cause-effect analysis, find out the list of the factors that influence client's perception of the software, weigh those factors, build a scorecard where those factors are used together with their weights to calculate the total performance, and finally get a number. Another approach is to form a group of users who have tried both software tools, and simply ask them, what is their preference.

Guess what option is easier to do? The second one! For sure, we will get a very subjective opinion about the software, but this approach works just fine, if we agree that the purpose of measurement is to find out what is the *preferred* choice.

When defining the purpose of measurement avoid vague definitions. Instead of formulating the purpose of measurement like "to get performance data" or "to estimate how we are doing" or "to improve outcomes," focus on 1-2 specific goals. Like in the example above we could define the purpose of measurement as vague as "To analyze the perceived quality of the software," but that purpose is too vague to serve for anything, so instead we focused on a specific goal: "Find out which of the two software tools is better perceived by the end-users."

Breaking down, stakeholders, purpose

Let's put these three processes together. Any measurement effort should be started with:

- Breaking-down big intangibles, into smaller tangible parts (decomposition)
- Defining people and systems that have interest (stakeholders)
- Defining the purpose of measurement (the context)

Examples

I suggest for the readers to review more examples below to get a sense of how powerful these three processes are.

Measuring Call Center Performance

Let's apply the three processes measurement prism described above to a Call Center. I will start with the stakeholders. These are:

- Clients who call
- Customer support staff who respond
- Managers
- Knowledge base system

What's the *purpose* of measurement? The first idea that normally comes into mind is "to improve the performance of the call center." For my opinion, this idea is too vague. To make it more specific we need to define what makes a call center successful. How about these success factors?

- Quick responses
- Providing effective solutions
- Low running costs

Is it a full list? No, we partially reviewed just one stakeholder (the client), but it is enough for this example. Now, we can define a more specific purpose for the measurement: "We want to measure how good our staff is in providing effective solutions to the clients." Let's do another turn and pass "effective solution" thought out the prism "subject – stakeholders – purpose:"

- **Subject**: Effective solution is one that works for the client, that doesn't require any additional clarification.
- **Stakeholders**: client, staff, knowledge base
- **Purpose**: keep more clients happy by giving effective solutions to their problems

How can we measure the effectiveness of the solutions? How about "Returning problems, %" metric? If a client contacted the call center, got a solution to his or her problem, but then the customer had to call again with the same problem, then something did not work well. The solution was not effective!

We can stop here, but I intentionally listed more stakeholders. One of the stakeholders is a representative of the call center. Does he or she have an influence on the effectiveness of the solution? Here are just few ideas:

- Probably the solution did not work, because the person who was analyzing the client's issue was not a good listener and was not able to diagnose the problem, or
- Probably the knowledge base that he or she used, was not good enough, or
- Probably the training (more stakeholders!) about the product was not that good.

We can pass these new inputs though and out the measurement prism "subject – stakeholders – purpose" again to find more metrics that might be useful in this context!

Measuring that a person is a good listener

Let's continue with the example above and take a different research direction: what does it mean to be a "good listener?" I have some ideas, but I guess there are a lot of experts on this topic who know this domain better than me. We can search in Google: "How to be a good listener" and we will find a lot articles on the topic. I did my search and the Harvard Business Review[8] article came up.

According to the authors, instead of being silent when others are talking, be a good listener and "periodically ask questions that promote discovery and insight." Can we quantify this? I guess it is possible, probably not in real time, and not for all conversations, but why not take a few conversations randomly, and ask an experienced staff person to review those conversations with the goal to estimate how well his or her colleague used opportunities to ask questions.

Should this new metric be included into the "Call center effectiveness index" indicator? It can be included in a certain position and certain weight. We will talk more about building scorecards in Step 5 of the KPI System.

Understanding leading factors is an art (Alcoa company)

With the examples described above the discipline of breaking down complex systems into more tangible parts and analyzing the leading factors might look like something easy to do, but in some sense this is an art.

Let's take the Alcoa company case that Jeroen de Flander describes in "The Execution Shortcut"[9]. Alcoa deals with a molten aluminum. When back in 1987, a new CEO Paul O'Neill came to the company, their injury rate per 100 worker per year was 1.86 (compare it to the national rate in US, which was at the level of 5 incidents per 100 workers). But to the surprise of the shareholders, the CEO decided to

---

[8] What Great Listeners Actually Do, Jack Zenger, Joseph Folkman, Harvard Business Review, 2016, https://hbr.org/2016/07/what-great-listeners-actually-do

[9] The Execution Shortcut: Why Some Strategies Take the Hidden Path to Success and Others Never Reach the Finish Line, Jeroen De Flander, the performance factory, 2013

focus their strategy not on improving shareholder results (at least not directly), but on **safety**.

Did it work? The safety data improved[10], but what is more important is that almost fanatical focus on safety also resulted in the improvement of the financial outcomes. Long story short: employees liked that the company started caring about them (not just on paper), and their engagement improved radically, a chain reaction was started and soon other performance outcomes improved as well.

I remember me reading this story in "The Execution Shortcut" and the first thought I had: "How can one possibly come up with such an obvious, but still brilliant idea?!" If "safety" worked for Alcoa, what might it be in your business? The quality of product or service? Or "happiness" like described in the mentioned above Zappos company? The ability to find the important leading factors for your strategy might be supported by some business methods, but in general cases it is an art.

On the Step 7 of the KPI System we will talk more metrics that might be good candidates for the keystone indicators. The best advice that I can give now: make sure that the best members of your team have free time to think about what is value for the stakeholders and how it is created.

Measuring value

I gave this advice as a closing word on some of the workshop, and before attendees were heading to the coffee machines, someone asked: "Value created for the customers... Sounds good! Can we measure it?!"

Yes, we can. In this case we need to pay higher attention to the "Customers" in the list of stakeholders, as there are actually different groups of customers:

---

[10] Back in 2015 the company published their safety data in real-time on their website. At the time of writing this book they replaced it with "Alcoa Sustainability" report, http://www.alcoa.com/sustainability/en/pdf/Alcoa-Sustainability.pdf

- Those who pay for your product
- Those who might pay for your product, if you will change it
- Those who tried your product, but will never pay for it

We can use additional classification for the paying customer by the functions that they use in your product:

- They use all functions of your product
- They use only certain functions of your product
- They use your product not as you have expected

Dan Kennedy, a guru of info business, once shared a story. Author of the info product created a version 2.0 and decided to sell an upgrade to all those who bought version 1.0. The condition was to send back the materials (it's an old case, so the product was recorded on video cassettes) of version 1.0. To the surprise of the author a certain percent of materials arrived in the original unopened package. This story is not about procrastination, but to illustrate how little we sometimes know about our customers. If you suspect that something similar might be happening in your business, add an additional group:

- They paid for your product, but don't use it

The main point of this exercise is to put yourself into the shoes of your customer (different groups of the customer) or at least try to imagine what's on their mind. You could simply ask them, but in the most cases you won't get any good answer.

For example, authors of Playing to Win[11] talked about the approach that companies like P&G used to compare baby diapers. For a long time the industry standard metric was the volume of water that a diaper can absorb. However, for moms who do shopping that was not the decision-making factor – the value for them was formed by other

---

[11] Playing to Win: How Strategy Really Works, A. G. Lafley, Roger L. Martin, Harvard Business Review Press, 2013

factors, such as easiness to use, design, and some tactile sense of the material. That was not something that various focus groups could possible detect.

The best advice in the context of understanding is that the value that is created for a customer is to be the customer yourself, or at least be next to your customer. Still, this is not a guarantee that all aspects of value will be discovered, but I'm sure that if no one in your company plays this role, then you will be losing marketing positions.

Example: Measuring risk

Another challenging task is measuring "risk." There are many definitions of risk, and respectively many approaches to risk management. If you are looking for a starting point to add risk indicators to your scorecard, use the approach described below.

What do we need to know to measure a risk? Two things:

- Estimate the probability
- Estimate the impact

Let's take "Risk of missing a call from a prospective customer" as an example. How can there be an impact estimated? We know an average shopping cart value, so we can do an assumption that if the client will be lost due to the missed call our financial impact on average will be equal to the average shopping cart value. There of course is an impact on the company's brand and other things, but let's keep it simple. For example, the impact is $320. What about probability? Using data about waiting time in the call center we can get an idea about probability figures, how about 5%?

How can we use this data? For example, we can find out the financial representation of the risk by multiplying the impact on the probability: $320*5%= $16, we can use this data when deciding if we want to hire additional sales representatives to decrease the possibility of this risk, or decide if it is low enough now.

If approaching the risk in this way we convert the task of risk measurement into:

- Task of measuring the impact of the risk event, and
- Task of measuring the probability of the risk event

According to my practice, if formulated in this way, the task of measuring risk looks more tangible for most typical business cases.

Measurement prism won't work for vague goals and buzz words

As with any tool, the measurement prism has its working range. The main limitation of the measurement prism is that it won't help when the purpose of measurement is formulated vaguely, unrealistically, or by using buzz words. On the scorecard, the purpose of the measurement might be presented by a business goal, action plan, or some supporting documentation. Whatever the form is - avoid formal, meaningless definition of the purpose of measurement. In this section, I'm sharing some typical bad practices and give some ideas about how to avoid these cases.

"Keep an eye on it" is not an action plan

Sometimes when you ask a client "why do you have this indicator on your scorecard?" the answer is that "we will keep an eye on it and if something is changing we will react." It's not an action plan, your automation software can do it without your active participation. In the most cases those indicators were not the product of the discussion, and most likely were copied from some long list of KPIs on the Internet without any particular idea about how it will help the company. Find a better reason to have this indicator on your scorecard or just remove it.

Avoid heavy business jargon and vague goals

Pay an attention to what language you use to formulate your action plan. Avoid using buzz words, heavy business jargon and vaguely formulated goals. For example: "We are going to leverage growth opportunities via achieving excellence in leadership" sounds smart, but basically it says nothing to the person who will be working on the problem:

- What does "leverage growth opportunities" mean?
- What will be a "leverage?"
- Do we know what those "opportunities" are?
- What exactly do we mean by "leadership"?
- Do we have a measure for excellence in leadership?

Avoid milestone goals

For example, "Implement a new CRM within 1 year" is a milestone goal. In the end of the year you can give a "yes/no" answer to the question if the CRM was implemented. A better option could be to focus on some change goal like "Improve efficiency of customer support" with "implement a new CRM" as one of the initiatives for that goal. Of course, you need to explain how the efficiency is defined in your case.

Don't mix goals and metrics

For example, "Improve customer engagement by 10%" is a mix of a goal ("Improve engagement") and a metric (an engagement index measured in percent). A better way to formulate this would be to define a goal and a metric separately. A goal can be "Improve customer engagement," a metric might be "Engagement index."

Avoid "Double something" goal

The goals where a company plans to double or triple something in the next year are supposed to motivate teams, but practice shows that these goals sounds unrealistic and have an opposite effect on the motivation. A goal "increase something by 48.5%" sounds more realistic as hopefully this "48.5" number is not a random one, but is the result of some analysis and is supported by a carefully developed action plan.

Avoid goals with undefined terms

Goals like "Increase productivity," "Improve performance," "Offer better value for money" don't look specific enough. What exactly do we mean by "productivity," "value," and "performance" in this case? Do you have a good metric that will give you a number for "productivity" or "value?" If not, you need to find those metrics first. The KPI System will help to do this!

Step 2. Scorecard checklist - detecting blind spots

In Step 2 we will talk about the pitfalls and bad practices related to the domain of measurement. Use these ideas as a checklist to revise your scorecard regularly and detect metrics that due to changing business environment became less useful. The examples discussed below will help to adjust your radar for the bad metrics and will help to find better ones.

2.1. Metrics without context

The process described in Step 1 implies that metrics that are used on the performance scorecards have some meaning for the business, e.g. there is some business context for those metrics. Sometimes managers find some interesting-sounding metric on the Internet and cannot resist a temptation to copy it their scorecard.

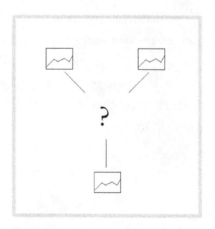

Example: "Revenue Per Employee"

2.1   Metrics without context

Let's take "Revenue Per Employee" as an example. The indicator shows the sales generated by one employee. It is good to know how productive your staff is, isn't it? They say, if you know something, but don't act on it, then you actually don't know it… So, why stop here? We can increase the "productivity" of the employees by setting a higher target for "Revenue Per Employee!" That's what real management is!

I hope readers can recognize my ironical tone, I don't think this approach to the indicator was useful, on the contrary, by this innocent experiment we have created some potential problems:

- **Motivational problem**. We showed in this way how we estimate the value of an employee – by measuring the revenue he or she generates. Did we really take into account all the long-term influence of building a good relationship with customers? No!

- **Strategy problem**. We do have a target, but we don't have a clue about how to achieve it - we don't have either an action plan or a strategy for it.

- **Alignment problem**. Even if there is a strategy, by design it will not be aligned with the other parts of the strategy. We just picked a random indicator and now are trying to find a good fit for it in our business.

Don't misunderstand me, I'm not saying that "Revenue per employee" is a bad metric. I'm saying that the described "metric to goal" approach might work, but in the most cases it does more harm than good. How can we do better? One needs to start with a business context first, look for the metrics that will help to address certain business goals, and only then start looking for the performance indicators.

Example: "HR Turnover Rate"

Another typical example of a KPI without proper business context is "Turnover rate, %" from the domain of talent management. Once this indicator appears on the HR's dashboard strange thing happens – for some reason managers start considering high turnover rate to be indicator of bad hiring and management practices. As a result, the HR strategy starts building around the ways to keep turnover rate low. Everything looks logical until someone asks a question:

- "Do we retain talented high performers in the company or do we just retain people to keep turnover rate low?"

Let's take the Apple company as an example, Apple is considered to be a great place to work, so they can choose a different strategy[12], instead of trying to keep everyone in the company they focused on better training and faster hiring approach. It makes more sense than just keeping the turnover rate low. If you need a better alternative for "Turnover rate," try "Turnover rate among high-performers."

2.2. Important goals without metrics

The opposite case of the previous situation is when there is some important goal on the company's strategy map, but there are no indicators aligned with it, or at least there are no good ones. Managers might argue that there are no indicators aligned with the goal, as that goal is not measurable, but as it was shown in the previous chapters, one can find an approach to quantify and measure anything.

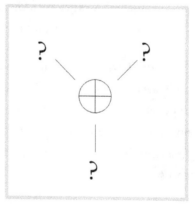

2.2   Important goals without metrics

The actual problem is that the subject of measurement (the goal and

---

[12] Apple's Employees Have A Hell Of A Ride, Steve Denning, 2012, Forbes

its context) is not studied well enough. That's fine if you are in the planning stage, but if you are about to start execution of your plan, make sure that proper indicators were found first.

2.3. Focusing on easy to measure, but low-value metrics

Guess what will happen if you, after reading the previous chapter, ask your team to find some metrics? The easiest and the most probable result is that you will find on your scorecard some easy to measure, but low-value metrics.

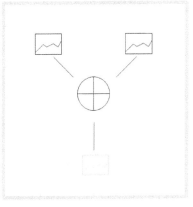

Let's take "Sales skills training" as an example. What do you think are the most popular metrics for this goal? Do a search on the Internet, and I'm sure you will find these two:

2.3   Low-value metrics

- Training time, hours
- Average exam score, %

Basically, by looking at these two metrics we say, that we care about time you spend in training class, and we care about how good you are at passing tests, but the rest is not our business. Easy to measure, but very basic metrics. Can we do better? Absolutely! See the "Training Scorecard and KPIs" in the Examples section for a more effective approach.

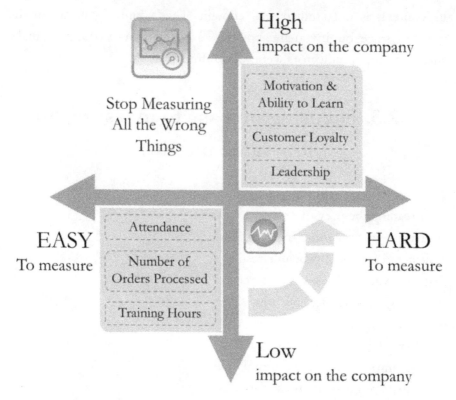

High
impact on the company

Stop Measuring
All the Wrong
Things

Motivation &
Ability to Learn

Customer Loyalty

Leadership

EASY
To measure

Attendance

Number of
Orders Processed

Training Hours

HARD
To measure

Low
impact on the company

Figure 6 Avoid focusing on easy to measure, but less useful metrics

Master your skill in detecting such low-value metrics. Practice shows that metrics that are related to the inputs of activity and to the results of the activity are the most risky ones in terms of their low worth for the performance measurement.

2.4. Observation error

Things around are always subject to change randomly. We all are human beings so we tend to credit these sudden changes (especially positive ones) with supporting our theories. Let's say we are tracking the number of website visitors and customer satisfaction on a weekly basis. Our marketing specialists started a new promo campaign and the next week we see that the number of visitors over time increased by 7%, and the customer satisfaction according to the online surveys, improved by 5% as well. Inspired by this success we go ahead with the campaign thinking that our decision is supported by data, but it is not. It was just some random fluctuation that we were not able to recognize.

We did this!

What should you do in this case? Do what scientists do when they observe something: they understand

2.4   Observation error

the changing nature of things, and they understand uncertainty of measurement methods. That's why in the scientific world any measurement goes with an observation error. The observation error in its turn includes random error (due to the changing nature of measured value, like website visitors in this case) and systematic error (due to the measurement tools used, like online surveys in this example).

Do you know what's the difference between the presentation of data on the business dashboards and the results that you would find in a scientific laboratory? On the business dashboard, you will see "75% customer satisfaction rate," and social scientists will use something like this "75%±10%," where 10% is an observation error. The estimated value for the observation error is not random and can be obtained using, for example, a set of several measurements. When we use 75% value on the business dashboard, we imply that there is an observation error, but it's easy to forget about this when validating the results of measurement, especially if they look like what we have expected.

2.5. Avoid narrow scope of measurement

Any measurement makes sense in a certain context, and it's important to understand this context in order to interpret the results correctly. For example, a CEO might credit the 10% increase in annual revenue to the success of executed strategy, when it is actually a market that was growing 20% a year, and a more objective interpretation is that in terms of market share, a company was losing its positions. The measurement scope in this case should be wider and take into account market trends as well.

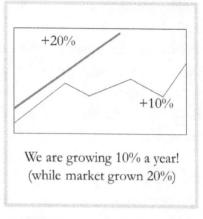

We are growing 10% a year! (while market grown 20%)

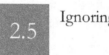 Ignoring Trends

In some cases it´s important to widen time horizon. We tend to ignore insignificant changes that happen every month, but try looking at them in a longer time horizon, and the data will be more frightening. How do you feel about losing 2% in the customer satisfaction index according to the latest monthly survey? "It is not that big to start worrying about," someone might say, or, "it is just a systematic error!" It may be, and to confirm a hypothesis of this we need to look not just at monthly, but at the annual data as well. Make sure your automation software helps you to analyze these trends.

2.6. Survival bias

The ultimate purpose of the performance measurement system is to help you improve your business, not just to validate what you have been doing. During World War II the Center for Naval Analyses studied bombers that returned to the base with the goal being to find the areas that required more armor. The data was collected and analyzed, and the suggestion was to armor areas with the highest amount of damages.

Statistician Abraham Wald applied different logic – if the plane was able to return to the base with those damages, then they are not critical ones. The critical damages were on those planes that did not return to the base, and respectively were not included in the analysis. That's known as "survival bias." Today a typical survival bias is that we like learning from the successful companies, with a hope to repeat their success, but what might be more interesting is to learn more actively from the companies that lost due to some reason.

We are very good at measuring how happy our happiest customers are

2.6   Survival bias

A similar situation is observed in the performance measurement. We are very good at measuring what we can see, but we are very short-sight in the context of "survival bias." Let's take customer satisfaction rate as an example, we get some number, let's say 75% and do an assumption that 75% of the customers are satisfied ones. The assumption is wrong, because we took into account only those customers who agreed to answer the questions on the customer survey. It's more correct to say that out of 100% of the customers who agreed to answer a few survey questions, 75% said that they will recommend the product to their friends, liked the product, will buy more, whatever... Aren't we missing something?

For example, those customers who decided not to spend a few minutes of their valuable time to respond to the questions? And of course there are even more prospective clients who were not interviewed because they simply have not bought anything from us. What do you think about 75% customer satisfaction rate now?

My recommendation is to be a professional skeptic about the measurements. Challenge your team with a survival bias case applied to your domain. Most likely you won't find any good metrics after the first try, but the discussion about what's not being captured by your measurement system, will be very fruitful.

2.7. Avoiding "bad news" indicators

This is another typical bias. Sometimes we don't place indicators on the scorecard, just because we know that it will be in the red zone, and for now we don't know what to do about it. Do a quick test: are there any indicators in the red zone on your scorecard? If no, then your team probably is affected by this bias as well.

2.7 Avoiding "bad news" indicators

If we have some strategy map with some goals on it and aligned indicators, then it is natural that in the beginning of the strategy execution process some of the indicators will be in the red zone. That's the point of any strategic goal: do things differently, and the indicator shows how we are progressing, there is nothing bad about it. But still many business professionals tend to avoid "bad news" indicators.

Technical solution for the "bad news" indicators

We faced this situation when working with the customers of BSC Designer software. Imagine a user who is tracking "Customer satisfaction, %" indicator. They start with as low as 30% customer satisfaction and want to improve it up to 75%. It's very demotivating to see a "customer satisfaction" indicator in the red zone every day, and we saw that people just moved this indicator to some private scorecard, where the boss doesn't see it at each board meeting. That's one option, but there is a technical trick that can help to address this issue.

The idea is to think separately about:

- Absolute performance figures and
- Progress in the context of the current plan.

For example, users can set a target for the next month to increase "Customer satisfaction, %" by 5%. If 35% customer satisfaction was achieved, then by the end of the month, user's progress will be 100%, while the performance will be just 35%. Everyone is happy: the boss can see that employees are doing good; employees can see that they did well last month, and know that they have more jobs to do in the next month.

Step 3. Map the constraints, success factors, and performance outcomes

In this chapter, we will talk about a framework that will help to generate some quick insights for good performance indicators. This framework can be used in the context of any process or business goal. We know that all processes, goals, and plans are unique, but still there are some common features: inputs, success factors, constraints, outputs of the activities, and expected performance results.

Framework application example

To illustrate how this framework can be used, let's take lead generation as an example. A company formulates some type of marketing message and chooses some type of media to deliver this message. The managers expect prospective clients (leads) to be coming, visiting their website, calling on the phone, revising their offer, and finally buying from the company. With this basic model in mind we can define:

- **Inputs**: marketing message, message views, leads generated
- **Success factors**: the quality of marketing message, reach rate of the media channel, the quality of incoming leads
- **Constraints**: the number of leads that one media channel can generate; leads that one sales representative can process efficiently

- **Activities**: leads processing
- **Performance outcomes**: hot leads that can be used for the sales funnel

Compare "Inputs" and "Success factors" – with inputs we are focusing on the *quantitative* aspects of the inbound resources and activities, while with the success factors, we are focusing on the *qualitative* aspects of those resources and activities.

3 BIRD'S-EYE LOOK
Constraints, Leading, and lagging indicators.

LEADING METRICS
Find success factors and distinguish them from other inputs.

LAGGING METRICS
Distinguish results valuable for the stakeholders from all other outputs and activities.

BOTTLENECKS METRICS
What is limiting the value that you can create for the stakeholders?

The same happens with the pair "Outputs" and "Performance outcomes." In terms of the outputs we deal with all of the results we can possibly get. In the contrast, with the "Performance outcomes" our focus is on what really matters in an analyzed business context.

What about "constraints?" For any goal or process, it is a good idea to understand what is limiting the system from performing even better. In this example, the company could probably achieve excellence in the marketing message that they use, but the real limiting factor is the number of the unique leads that the selected channel can generate. Having this model in mind, where should we focus our measurement efforts?

Measures for inputs and success factors

For any business challenge a good starting point is to understand the success factors, and find respective measures for them. Such metrics are also called "leading" indicators.

- **Leading indicators** are aligned with the success factors and help to predict that the expected results will be achieved.

In the lead generation example the leading indicators will be the ones that help to estimate the quality of the marketing message, the quality of the incoming leads, and their number. How can we quantify the "quality of marketing message?" We would need to return to the first step of the KPI System: define what quality is, who are the stakeholders, and what is the purpose of the measurement. The most challenging is the definition of the "quality" in this case. In some sense writing an appealing marketing message is an art, but it is also a technology. Do a Google search and you can easily find factors that could make your message a success:

- Appealing headline
- Message based on "problem + solution + result" formula
- Credibility of message

We can quantify on these parameters and measure the quality of the marketing message respectively. I know that some sceptics would argue: "That's good, but still there is not a guaranty that it will work!" You are right! In Step 4 of the KPI System we will talk about how to deal with something unknown from the viewpoint of measurement. A quick answer is: do experiments!

Success factors vs. leading indicators

One question that clients often ask is about the difference between the success factors (or critical success factors) and the leading indicators. As it was shown before, they are connected. Here is the main difference:

- Leading indicators are **quantitative** in their nature, while success factors are **qualitative**.

In simple words, the success factors specify the requirements (qualities) for the success, and the indicators tell us how successful we are in satisfying those requirements.

Activities' outputs and performance outcomes

What about the difference between the outputs of the activities and the performance outcomes?

- Outputs are the results of the activities (sorry for the cross reference)
- Performance outcomes are the outputs that are important for us in the defined business context

Remember what Ted Levitt said: "People don't buy a quarter-inch drill bit; they buy a quarter-inch hole." The "quarter-inch hole" is what is important for the person in that context; that's what is the "performance outcome" is in this case. Other activities of the drilling, like making noise, consuming electricity, and other outputs like shavings, are not that important.

Thinking about the performance measurement: where should we focus our measurement efforts? It depends on the context, on the purpose of measurement. The context defines what the simple outputs are and what are the performance outcomes. For example, the activity-related metrics might be useful if we need to optimize certain processes. If you plan to equip a joiner workshop and you are concerned about the environmental impact of the tools used, then your measurements will be related to the outputs like electricity consumption.

The same approach works for our marketing example. If your sales system is not adjusted to the new type of leads yet, then you will have to pay attention to the activity-based measures, such as processing time, resources involved, etc., and optimize them. Once the system is working properly the focus will be shifted to the expected results, e.g. the number of hot leads that were obtained from that media.

This type of metrics is called lagging indicator:

- **Lagging indicators** are aligned with the expected performance results and help to validate them in the certain business context.

What happens with the activity metrics? If you did it right in terms of automation (see Step 10 of the KPI System), then most of your activity metrics are obtained automatically from your business systems. Move those indicators to a separate operational dashboard, and keep an eye on them, especially when some important changes are introduced.

Constraints and bottlenecks

A constraint or a bottleneck is something that is liming the performance of your system. Any business has constraints, but it doesn't mean that the part of the business system that you are analyzing right now has such constraints. From the viewpoint of measurement that's the first point to look at.

- **Constrains indicators** are aligned with the aspects that are limiting the performance of the business system.

Money is not a good constraint

What is limiting your business? If the answer is "money" then most likely you did something wrong. Money is never a good limiting factor of a for-profit business. If you have a business that converts $100 into $100 + $1 profit (considering all management expenses, risks, and capital interests), then you can easily find investments for your business.

Look again at your business challenge, what is a real limit? The number of talented people, their productivity, limits of the marketing channels, or limits of your possibilities to growth?

Leading, lagging, constrain indicators

To summarize what was said before:

- Leading indicators help to predict the success
- Lagging indicators help to validate the achieved results
- Constrain indicators focus on what's limiting your system

Below is an action plan for dealing with these types of indicators.

Optimize on the constrains

First, find the constrains. Let's return to our example: imagine that the sales process is not optimized yet; there is not enough staff who can answer the phone; and those who answer are not able to answer the questions properly. That's the important constrain of the system! How can we improve the results in this case? You can certainly increase the number of incoming leads, but it will be similar to burning money. The first goal should be to eliminate the performance leaks inside your system by focusing on the constraint indicators, for example the "first call resolution rate" or "average waiting time."

Limits in the leading factors

What happens with the constrains when you have optimized your processes? There are still bottlenecks in your business, but the constraints of the business environment around your organization become much more important compared to the limits of your own system. In some sense the environmental constraints are aligned with the success factors for your business.

Returning to our example: when the constraints are optimized, you will see that your system can process most leads effectively, but the media channels that you use to deliver your message are not able to provide you with the right number of qualified leads and the goal would be to optimize on the success factors, e.g. find the media channel that generates better leads.

Lagging indicator bias

Lagging indicators help to validate the results. In our example finding lagging indicators is easy, as we will be able to see the performance outcomes quickly and we can also estimate them financially, for example using customer lifetime value data. In some cases, finding good lagging indicators is a tricky task. Let's use ROI (Return on Investment) as an example. This is a typical lagging indicator. The *investment* part is normally easy to calculate; the *return* part is what makes the most of the problems.

What about calculating ROI for the employee training? Believe me, measuring financial ROI is a tough task in this case. But what if we will redefine the purpose of the measurement? We assume that the value created for an employee will result in financial outcomes. Now, instead of measuring the financial outcomes we can measure the value created for the employees. Will it be an accurate measure? It won't. But it many cases we don't need a specific figure in dollars. For example, if the goal is to choose between two training offers we can do an initial estimation based on the value that it creates, not on the expected financial outcomes. In the "Examples" chapter you will find a "Training Scorecard' where we discuss in detail a possible approach to this challenge.

Quick example: leading, lagging, constraint indicators

Here is a quick example that helps you to remember the difference between leading and lagging indicators. Many people have a personal goal to lose weight. The *leading indicators* in this case will be everything related to the diet and exercise; the *lagging indicators* will be the weight; the *constraints* might be the maximum exercise load that one can do.

Step 4. Measuring unknown

Is there something that you still cannot measure?

What is the most challenging in the approach described above? I'd mention these aspects:

- **Leading factors bias.** We can recognize some factor as a reason for the success only when we have achieved that success. The business environment is changing constantly and by the time we know what the success factor was, we might not be able to reproduce the same situation exactly.
- **Lagging indicator timeframe.** As for the lagging indicators, the real performance results for them might come in decades and we simply don't have time to wait so long.

What can we do in these cases? Use two methods that scientists use: come up with a hypothesis, do observations and experiments.

Experiments

In the previous chapter, we were discussing a "marketing message quality" as one of the leading indicators. Let's imagine a situation that your marketing team knows nothing about writing appealing titles, focusing on the customer's value in the message, and implementing calls to action. How do we measure the success in this case?

Let's redefine the purpose of measurement a little bit: instead of understanding the best practices and improving on them, the new purpose is to understand what marketing message is working better.

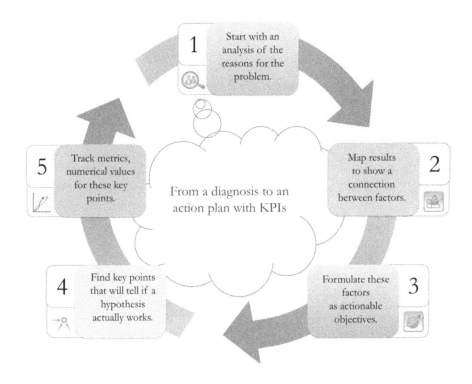

Figure 7 Testing hypothesis with KPIs

Let's do an experiment: ask marketing team to write three random marketing messages about your product. Post them on Google AdWords and see what message will be converting better into the clicks and into the sales. Choose the winner, and ask your team to rework it. Repeat the experiment with the new three candidates. Soon the winning option will be found.

This approach is not flawless, as for example, the found message is the best only in a certain range of the examined messages; probably there is one that is even better. But still, we achieved the purpose of the measurement. In many cases, instead of measuring things, it´s much easier to set up an experiment and see how people will react.

What's the problem with the experiments

In quantum mechanics, it is known as the Heisenberg uncertainty principle. By experimenting we are interfering with the subject of the experiment. To underline the artistic nature of the observation and the experiments, I´d like to share a story about Zhongli Quan, an immortal of Taoism[13]:

One day he noticed a woman who was sitting near a grave and fanning the soil. Such behavior looked strange to him, so he asked about the reason, and she told him that this was the grave of her husband, and she promised him not to remarry until the soil on his grave dries. When back home, Zhongli Quan shared this story with his wife. She started blaming the widow, and that aroused Zhongli Quan's suspicion; he decided to test her and assumed the shape of a handsome young man. Skipping poetical details, she failed the test.

What can we learn from that story? Observation is important and has its benefits, but we should also note that: testing is tricky! Was it in Zhongli Quan's wife's plans to look for a young man, or it was an experiment that provoked her behavior? Due to the uncertainty principle, we cannot answer these questions.

When setting up experiments in a business context make sure that you take into account this uncertainty principle.

---

[13] Chinese Symbolism and Art Motifs: A comprehensive Handbook, Charles Alfred Speed Williams, Tuttle Publishing, 2006

UNKNOWN
Is there something that you still cannot measure?

OBSERVATION

Teach your team to read
between the lines

Look for the absence of
something

CONTROLLED
EXPERIMENTS
By experimenting we are
interfering with the subject of the
experiment

Observation

In some sense observation is much safer that the experiments, as the risk of interfering with the subject of observation is considerably low. Some argue that by just observing things we cannot learn much about them... I would not agree, let's take discoveries in astronomy as an example. Most of them were made without direct interaction with the subjects of measurement. Moreover, some discoveries were made even without direct observation: for example, black holes can be observed only indirectly via their influence on matter nearby.

In the business context "observation" is an ability to be with your client and read between the lines when needed. I believe in your team there are people who have mastered these skills, so make sure that their opinion counts when the organizational strategy is formulated and executed.

Limits of the KPI System

Can anything be quantified and measured? Let's have a look at the Cynefin framework, it offers a matrix with four domains - Simple, Complicated, Complex, and Chaotic. Thinking about the problems of measurement in the context of these four domains we can probably conclude that the measurement system won't make sense in "Simple" and "Chaotic" domains.

Let me illustrate this idea in the context of a presentation talk. Here are the examples of some metrics, and respectively the domains that they might belong to:

- "Air volume, m3" metric. In the defined context of the presentation talk, this is a metric from the "Simple" domain. We can certainly measure it, but in most cases, we could hardly link it to any business challenge.

- "Room occupancy rate, %" metric is a good fit for "Complex" domain, it is easy to calculate a current value for this metric by using data about the number of seats and the number of attendees.

- "Engagement rate, %" metric is a good candidate for the domain "Complicated", and after a series of probes and mistakes we can probably come up with some engagement metrics that will work in this case.

- What about the "Chaotic" domain, in this case the measure would be focused on something unpredictable. Imagine that during your presentation to a small client, a top manager of a Fortune 100 company accidentally enters the room and decides to buy your product, a metric can be something like "sales by chance, %."

In the business context that we agree upon, the "air volume, m3" metric from the "Simple" domain doesn't make any sense. The "sales by chance, %" metric from the "Chaotic" domain is a good match for the business context, but due to unpredictable nature of the measurement subject it won't be useful for us either.

What can we do about metrics in the "Chaotic" domains? We need to convert a chaotic situation into a "complicated" one. For example, the probability to get "sales by chance" increases significantly if you will discuss the details with your colleagues in a public space, like a cafe, especially if it is in the business center of the city.

The described approach might be used to categorize the metrics that you have on your scorecard. Some of them need to be removed as too obvious, some of them can be redefined.

Step 5. Setting up metric

In this chapter, we will discuss some technical details about how to set up metrics and group them into the scorecards. In practice this is a job for automation software, but before automating things, I'd recommend getting an idea about the supporting principles.

To illustrate the ideas of this chapter I'd like to introduce a new example. Imagine that we need to measure the performance of the *customer service*. What indicators would we need? To answer this question, we would need to start with Step 1 of the KPI System: use Measurement Prism and get a list of metrics. For the purpose of this example, I'll skip the discovery stage and get directly to the list of the indicators:

- First-contact resolution rate, %
- Time to answer customer emails, hours
- Customer satisfaction, %
- Average monthly load per agent, requests/agent
- Revenue per agent, $/agent
- Running costs per agent, $/agent

How can we summarize the data from these indicators in order to calculate the performance of the customer service? Here are some preparatory steps that we need to do:

1. Define the performance thresholds for the indicators. For example, for the "Time to answer customer emails" indicator the thresholds might look like this: green zone - "emails answered within 2 hours"; yellow zone - "emails answered within 8 hours"; red zone - "emails answered within more than 8 hours."

2. Define the performance formula and the optimization direction for the performance. In other words, we need to answer the

question of do we want to minimize the value of the indicator or maximize it? Obviously, we need to maximize "customer satisfaction," but minimize "time to answer emails."

3. Define the relevant importance (weights) of the indicators. All of the mentioned indicators have an influence on the customer service differently. For example, it is important to respond to emails quickly ("time to answer emails" indicator), but it is even more important that the response is effective (measured by "first-call resolution rate").

Let's discuss in detail each of these preparatory steps.

5.1. Thresholds and measurement scale

We can use some color-based thresholds with red, yellow, and green colors like described above. The problem with these types of thresholds is that we will still need to digitalize them if we want to use them in the calculations. A better approach is to define a measurement scale first, and then assign a certain color threshold (or a stoplight) to the particular performance values.

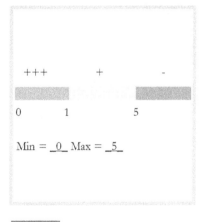

5.1   Measurement scale

Standard scale

What can be a measurement scale for the mentioned customer service indicators? Sometimes the scale is defined by the type of measurement, for example the possible range for the first-call resolution rate is between 0% and 100%. 110% first-call resolution, as well as negative rate don't make any business sense.

To indicate the ranges for the scale we defined 0 as its minimal value, and 100 as its maximal value. I'll use [min...max] notation for the scale:

- First-call resolution rate, %. Scale: [0...100]%

Negative scale

Another indicator that is measured in percent is "Customer satisfaction, %." The scale for this indicator depends on how we define the indicator itself. For example, if it is the percent of satisfied customers, then we can define measurement scale as [0...100]. In this case, we only counted the positive responses in the customer survey. That's the most used approach to measuring customer satisfaction, but theoretically we can also take into account all responses, including negative ones. In this case if all of the customers say that they are dissatisfied, we will have a negative customer satisfaction -100%. This example illustrates that sometimes a measurement scale is not that obvious. I suggest following the classical approach with [0...100] scale:

- Customer satisfaction, % Scale: [0...100] %

Scale and the business context

We have to choose a scale for the other three indicators. For the "Time to answer customer emails, hours" we need to choose some realistic scale in hours. Theoretically it is possible to answer emails as fast as in 10 seconds after a sender has sent it, and sometimes it takes weeks to answer a client's requests (some of that governmental organizations answer even slower!). The idea here is to choose the scale that makes sense in your business context. For example, on average your company answers emails within 24 hours, but during holidays the response time might be longer. In this case you have two options:

1. Select a scale that corresponds to your case, for example [0...48] hours, or
2. Split the "Time to answer" indicator into indicators "Time to answer during open hours" and "Time to answer during weekends"

If you want to achieve excellence in customer service, I'd focus on the second approach. Inside "Time to answer customer emails, hours" we now have:

- "Time to answer during open hours", scale [0...24] and
- "Time to answer during weekends", scale [0...48]

Scale and historical values

In our example, we have two more indicators without a scale. To find a scale for them, I'd suggest using minimal and maximal historical values for that indicator:

- Running costs per agent, $/agent, scale [50...480]$
- Revenue per agent, $/agent, scale [0...7480]$
- Average monthly load per agent, requests/agent, scale [0...200] requests/agent

5.2. Define performance formulas and optimization direction

At this stage, we need to understand how we are going to calculate the performance of the indicator. Let's take this one for example:

- "Time to answer during open hours," scale [0...24]

If it took 24 hours to answer a short email from a client, then what was the performance of the customer service? Was it 0% or 100%? Obviously, on the scale [0...24] hours, the answer in 24 hours is the longest possible answer time and the performance is 0%.

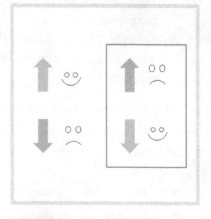

Another example, what about this indicator:

- "Revenue per agent," scale [0...7480]$?

5.2   Optimization direction and performance

If an agent generated $7480 this month is the performance low or high? Obviously, on the selected scale the agent performed 100%.

If thinking about the performance as a linear function of the current value, then in the first case where we wanted to minimize an indicator's value (lower value means higher performance) we would use this performance formula:

$$Performance\ (minimization), \% = \frac{max - value}{max - min} * 100\%$$

In the second case where we needed to maximize the value of the indicator (higher value means higher performance) the formula would be this one:

$$Performance\ (maximization), \% = \frac{value - min}{max - min} * 100\%$$

What's the benefit of calculating the performance?

After doing some calculations, instead of dealing with different measurement units (like "hours," "$/agent," "%," "Requests/agent") we can now deal with only one – with the "percent!" It means that we can compare two indicators that were not comparable before! Try comparing "5 hours response time" and "$200 revenue generated by agent" – it's not possible, but if we set a measurement scale for both indicators, we can calculate the performance in percent for both, and now we can compare them.

Another benefit is that now we know what we want to do with the value of the indicator. We want to minimize or maximize it, and we don't require any additional clarification in this context.

What if performance is not a linear function

In some cases, the performance is not a linear function of the value. Let's take workload of sales agent as an example. Depending on the nature of business, there is a certain number of clients that sales agent can process efficiently and effectively. Let's say this number is 8 clients per day. How could we calculate the performance of a sales agent in this case? If there are just 2 clients per day, then the agent's load is not enough and we are losing money, if the work load is 14 clients, then we are losing money as well, because the sales agent cannot process all those leads well.

The performance function is this case might be something like this:

$$Performance\ (sine\ function) = \sin \frac{value - min}{(max - \min) * \pi}$$

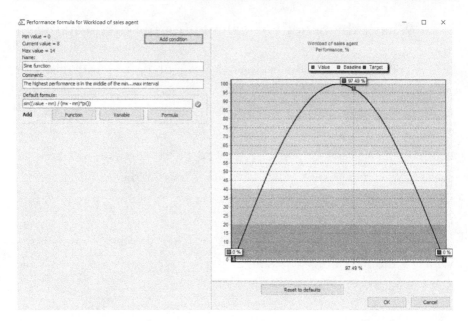

Figure 8 An example of a nonlinear performance function

And the visual representation of the current indicator performance on the gauge diagram would like this one:

Figure 9 An example of the gauge diagram for the indicator with nonlinear performance

As mentioned before, all these formulas here are for the illustration purposes only. I'm not arguing that you should do the calculations manually– you have an automation software for this. For example, users of BSC Designer will find a choice of some standard performance formulas and the possibility to add their own.

Progress calculation

The described approach to calculating the scorecard is implemented in most software tool for the automation of the scorecards. However, the practical use of this approach revealed one potential problem when tracking the performance.

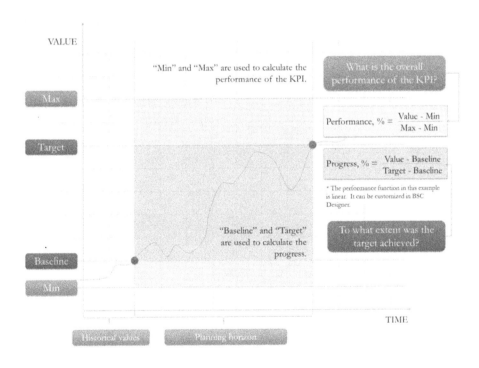

Figure 10 The difference between performance and progress

Imagine that you are measuring "Customer satisfaction, %" indicator on the scale [0...100%] with the current customer satisfaction value equal to 75%. Your goal for the next month is to achieve at least

78% satisfaction. In terms of the measurement scale [0…100%] it is just 2% improvement, but for your team it might mean doing a huge amount of work to do this. Another problem is that if your team does nothing, the performance of the indicator will still be 75%, and that's still a good level. To avoid these issues, managers and team members need to see the progress on a more tangible scale.

There is a need for a tool that would help to measure the performance change in a shorter time horizon. We could create a separate "Progress" indicator, but in this case, we'd have to duplicate all other data. A better solution is to align progress data directly with the indicator. To do this we will need to define an additional scale [baseline…target].

The baseline is a starting point for the improvement, in this case it is 75%; and the target (another option is to use "benchmark" word) is an expected value, which is 78%. Now we have a [0...100]% scale for the performance, and a [75...78]% scale for the progress. After a month of hard work your team will see two numbers: 78% performance; and if they have beaten the 78% target they will also see 100% progress.

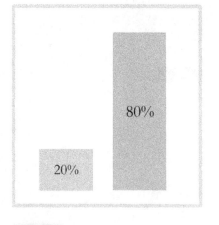

5.3. Define weight

Let's get back to the previously defined constructions. We have a "container" indicator: "Time to answer customer emails, hours" that includes two sub-indicators:

5.3　Weight of the indicator

- "Time to answer during open hours", scale [0...24] and
- "Time to answer during weekends", scale [0...48].

Using some sample data, we can calculate the performance of both indicators:

- "Time to answer during open hours", scale [0...24], current value = 3 hours; performance = 87.5%
- "Time to answer during weekends", scale [0...48], current value = 21 hours; performance = 56.25%

For the calculations, I've used a "Performance (minimization)" formula that was discussed before, and the scale of measurement as it was defined for two indicators. What should the performance of the "container" indicator "Time to answer customer emails, hours" be? We can calculate it as an average of the indicators inside the container:

$$Container\ performance = \frac{87.5 + 56.25}{2} = 71.88\%$$

Let's focus now on another pair of indicators and assume that their current performance is as follows:

- First-call resolution rate, %, current performance = 51.00%
- Time to answer customer emails, hours, current performance 89.58%

What if we calculate the performance of customer service using only these two indicators? I'm applying the same formula for average and the result is:

$$Customer\ service\ performance = \frac{51 + 89.58}{2} = 70.29\%$$

The math is correct, but if thinking about this results in the business context I would say that something is wrong: in terms of a quick answer to the emails, we are doing good (89.58%), but in terms of "The first-contact resolution rate" there is a problem, as only 51% of questions are resolved within the first contact. I would expect the overall performance not to be as high as 70.29%. In other words, "Response time" indicator is important for the performance, but "First-contact resolution rate" is more important. To take this idea into account we need to introduce additional coefficients (weights) to the performance of sub-indicators.

Let's assume that the weight of the "First-contact resolution rate" indicator is 80% and the weight of "Response time" indicator is 20%. In this case the container performance will be:

$$Container\ weighted\ performance = 0.8 * 51 + 0.3 * 89.58$$
$$= 58.72\%$$

This "weighted" performance makes much more sense now. In the same way, weight can be applied to all levels of the scorecard. If you are interested in learning all of the formulas that can be used for the calculation of weight on different levels of scorecard, I'd recommend checking out the details in "Scorecard and KPIs 101" article published on bscdesigner.com.[14]

5.4. Technical details checklist

Finally, don't forget that for your new metric you need to define its name, description and set targets for specific dates. The goal is to make sure that for all members of your team the metric is unambiguously identified, and it is clear how exactly the current value for the metric will be obtained. To summarize the chapter, here is a short checklist for the scorecard calculations:

- Define a scale for measurement

---

[14] Scorecard and KPIs 101: Calculation of Indicators, Aleksey Savkin, http://www.bscdesigner.com/scorecard-and-kpis-101.htm, 2014, BSC Designer

- Define performance function (linear maximization or minimization)
- Define weights of the indicators
- Calculate the performance and, if needed, progress
- Define metric name and description
- Set targets for specific dates

Step 6. Prioritizing indicators on the scorecard

After passing the previous steps of the KPI System you will have a long list of metrics. In this chapter, we will talk about how to prioritize your measurement efforts.

SORTING METRICS
How do you prioritize indicators on your scorecard?

	URGENT	NOT URGENT
IMPORTANT	Operational goals and their metrics	Strategic goals and their metrics
NOT IMPORTANT	Something to outsource to the scorecard of other department	Why do you still have these goals and metrics on your scorecard?

Let's use a decision matrix also known as Eisenhower's matrix. We have two axes and a four-sector diagram. The axes are *Urgency* with two options – Urgent and Not Urgent; and *Importance* with two options – Important and Not Important. Respectively, the four sectors of the diagram are: Urgent and important; Urgent, but not important; Not urgent, but important; Not urgent, not important.

Let's have a look at the list of the metrics and sort them into these four categories:

- "Not urgent, not important" – the candidates that you should get rid of right now.
- "Urgent, but not important" – in this case we are normally talking about metrics that are out of your direct control, someone in your team should track them, but probably not you;

consider "outsourcing" these metrics and respective goals/processes to your colleagues

- "Urgent and important"- operational metrics, these are probably metrics related to your current business challenges
- "Important, but not urgent" – strategic metrics, the ones that are aligned with the strategic goals.

Strategic vs. operational metrics

Before we discussed the three different types of metrics – leading, lagging, and constraint metric. How do these types fit into this four-sector model? Are they strategic or operational? The word "strategic" became a buzzword that normally means that we are talking about something long-term, something suggested by the top managers. I prefer a more practical definition. Here is the difference between operational and strategic goals:

- **Operational goal** is about doing things right (improving on best practices)
- **Strategic goal** is about doing right things or doing things differently, changing the way you approach the challenge.

A strategic metric, is one that is aligned with a strategic goal as it is defined above, and a respectively operational metric is one that is aligned with the operational goals.

Let's take product training as an example. One way to teach your clients to use your product is to run training sessions. The operational goal in this case might be formulated as "decrease training costs," and "increase effectiveness of the training." To track the progress towards these goals we can use such metrics as:

- Training time, hours
- Trainees satisfaction rate, %

- Trainees engagement, %
- Average exam score
- Travel and accommodation costs

By using these metrics we are trying to do exactly the same things we did before, but to do them better. A strategic goal in this case could be something related to approaching differently the challenge of training clients to use your product. Instead of making a focus on the live training sessions, the organization might be introducing some of the training materials in the form of prerecorded video lessons. The key challenge might be to make the video materials more engaging and informative compared to the old-style training. The metrics in this case will be different:

- Lagging metric: Usage of video materials per trainee, hours
- Leading metric: Product features covered by the video materials, %

The changed goal in this case is about switching from an old training model that implies travelling and face-to-face training to the new model based on video training. Instead of trying to optimize the old practices (this would be an operational goal), the focus is on trying a different approach.

An example: improving user manual vs. improving product

One of our clients was challenged by the metrics for the documentation of a software product. Many times, the clients of that organization reported that it was hard to understand the product manuals, and instead of solving the problem themselves, they had to contact customer service. After a short examination, we realized that the problem was not with the documentation itself, but with the interface of the product. It was far from being intuitive. Instead of focusing on metrics for the readability of documentation, we suggested focusing on the metrics for the software interface itself.

We asked the vendor to define several typical use cases, and to do a quick estimation of the ease of doing them, and by counting the number of clicks that a user should do to complete the task. This quick estimation showed that the software had too many options, and end users had to pass through most of them to get to what they needed.

The interface of the product was updated, and when the actualizations were installed on the users' side, it appeared that the number of requests regarding certain features decreased to almost zero. The lesson that we can learn from this example is that in many cases the best solution to the problem is not to solve it directly, but to do a root-cause analysis, and to find out the strategic (change) challenge that stands behind it. In the next chapter I will share some specific recommendations about how to do this.

Step 7. Find good leading and change metrics

"Thus the highest form of generalship is to stifle the enemy's plans; the next best is to prevent the joining of the enemy's forces; the next in order is to attack the enemy's army in the field; and the worst policy of all is to besiege walled cities."

Sun Tzu, The Art of War

I hope another quote of Sun Tzu will help to shift your mindset to the strategic tone... The use of strategic (=change) metrics has its own benefits:

- We could fix more problems in the products before users face them
- We could prevent more safety accidents before they produce too much damage
- We could prevent unwanted behavior before it happens
- We could try new hypothesis and achieve new results

In this chapter we discuss some starting points for your research.

FIND LEADING METRICS

How to find strategic (change) goals and metrics for them

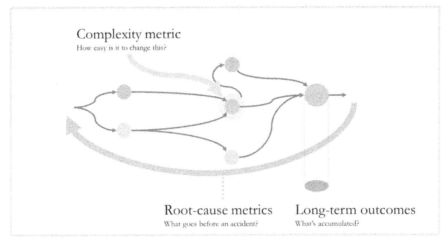

Complexity metric

How easy is it to change this?

Root-cause metrics   Long-term outcomes

What goes before an accident?   What's accumulated?

An example: root-cause metric

The basic approach is a root-cause analysis of the challenge. There is no one size fits all formula for root-cause analysis. I'm going to share some typical directions to look at. Let's take a safety accident as an example. What measures can we use to decrease the number of safety accidents?

We can measure the "number of critical safety accidents." A classical "X days without accidents" is an example of the realization of such an approach. It has a certain motivational effect, but when an accident has happened, it's too late.

What is causing critical safety accidents? The minor accidents! Why not build a metric on them: "The number of minor safety accidents (near miss accidents)." What is causing the minor safety accidents? Lack of certain training, safety procedures? In this case, we could focus measurement efforts onto different metrics like "% of workers who passed safety trainings" and "Implementation rate of safety procedures."

Still, even if these indicators are in the green zones, safety accidents might happen. The question is why? The answer is: a certain work culture. What is a culture and how can we measure it? A culture is a set of certain behavior patterns. What behavior pattern could indicate the higher risk of safety accidents? Probably we should track if someone is not wearing a uniform, or if that someone is using smartphone.

On a certain level the safety indicators might look very naive to the outsiders, but they work. If you want to learn more about improving safety, check out the Alcoa story discussed above. Their approach to safety was proactive: even minor safety accidents were reported; in a short period, a prevention plan should have been proposed. Can an organization *guarantee* that serious accidents won't happen? No! But the probability can be decreased significantly.

The question that we constantly asked in the previous case was: "What goes before..."

- What goes before a critical safety accident? Minor accidents...
- What goes before a minor safety accident? Safety procedures...
- What makes safety procedures successful?

Don't look just for the direct cause-and-effect connections, instead look at the factors that might be influencing them.

Back in 1982, social scientists James Wilson and George Kelling introduced their *broken windows theory*. They proved empirically that preventing minor crimes like vandalisms helps to prevent more serious crimes. What are the "broken windows" in your case? You know a lot about the challenge that you are facing right now. What was preceding this challenge? Ask this question to your team, and be ready to write down interesting insights.

An example: the number of mistakes

Here is another basic example of how a leading metric can be found. Let's take the quality of this book as a context. How can you find the number of typos in the book? We cannot know this for sure, but we can come up with an estimated value.

I was doing this when proofreading the written materials myself. I read the chapter and corrected all sort of the problems that I faced. Let's say after the first proofread I've fixed 8 problems. Does it mean that I found and fixed everything? Probably not. I read the chapter once more and fixed 2 more problems. Finished now? Probably, if I had the patience, I could read it until no problems were found. Was I able to fix all problems? No! But I hope a professional proofreader will help me to find what I have missed.

An example: complexity metric

In many cases the challenges that we face today are caused by the architecture that we designed yesterday. The architecture is too complex and too hard to maintain, and this leads to some unpredictable problems. How can we measure the complexity? Here is a quick complexity measure: try to change something and track the efforts your team need to do this.

Here is a short story in this context. A company was working on the new version of their software product, they hired a talented engineer who was supposed to add some new features to the software. Instead of doing what he was asked, he said:

- "I've noticed there is one field in the database table that doesn't sound like a descriptive one. Could we please first change the name of this field to a better one?"

Old team had to say that is it was not possible, because they would need to update field names in many cases, and this would probably generate some new bugs in the software. The new developer then said:

- "If we cannot introduce this small change, how can we possibly introduce the new feature that you asked me about?!"

That's a good question to ask! Before you plan to change your business system, make sure there are no complexity problems.

An example: what's accumulating in your business?

One day that was an eye-opening question for me: "What do you accumulate in your business?" Is there anything tangible that your business is accumulating each year? It's not just about the days your company exists and work hours. Think about something that has a value for you, it can be a user base with loyal clients or active clients paying subscriptions every month.

Can an "intellectual property" be your answer? It depends, it's not about the number of trademarks you register, it's about their market value. It's not about the number of lines of code that your software engineer wrote, it's about market potential of this product.

In some sense the answer to this question is what your business is in a nutshell. If you don't like the answer, then probably you don't like the current model of your business. Do you need a good strategic goal? Think about the ways to increase significantly the value that is accumulated. It would not be a surprise for me if when thinking about the accumulated assets you end up reinventing your perception of value.

Reverse thinking example: innovations

Here is a good example of how the leading metrics can be formulated in the domain of innovations. The lagging part of the innovations is relatively clear, we can measure the number of innovative initiatives that became successful in some time or measure their financial impact. But what about the leading part? How can we predict that the company will create these innovations?

What company will never innovate?

Let's formulate the opposite question: what is a profile of a company that most likely **won't be able** to innovate? These are the companies where: all new ideas are rejected, the barrier for approving new ideas is too high, the bureaucracy dominates over common sense, where short term profits are more important that long-term value for the customers, where employees are always busy with firefighting and simply don't have free time to think about something new, and where informational silos limit the exchange of information between the departments... We can go ahead and list more behavior patterns that have negative influence on the innovative potential. My point is that the innovative companies will do exactly the opposite things.

Do you need to measure how innovative your company is? Quantify and measure those behavior patterns. Don't forget about the stakeholders. Who might suggest an innovation? Employees, partners, clients? Are the members of your team using your product or service as end-users? How actively can your team experiment? There are always some good ideas out there, the question is if you team has the time and resources for the experiments.

How innovative is your environment?

The basic metrics might be:

- The number of ideas suggested by the team over a period of time
- The percent of the ideas turned into experiments
- Dedicated time for the experiments

Where do those ideas come from? In the previous chapter, we agreed to divide inputs and success factors, but the inputs always correlate in some way with the success factors.

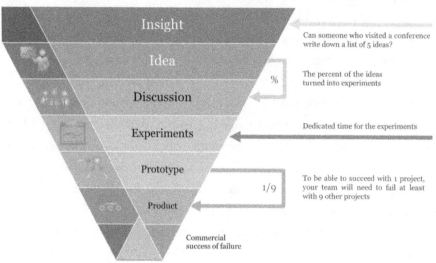

Figure 11 Innovation funnel

What might be the inputs for the innovation? Do the members of your team read the books in their domain, visit conferences? Can we expect that someone who visited a conference can write down a list of 5 ideas that your team can try later? That's easy if someone watched the presentations and networked with colleagues!

Innovation funnel

Having discussed how the companies innovate (and don't innovate) we can build an innovation funnel. It will be something like: insight > idea > discussion > experiments > prototype > product > commercial success of failure.

If you ask any entrepreneur about the number of his or her successful projects, you would hear something like 3 of 10 projects fail, 6 of 10 are poor performers, 1 of 10 is where we can achieve excellence. What do these numbers tell us in terms of innovation? To be able to succeed with 1 project, your team will need to fail at least with 9 other projects. And make sure your teams are really trying and not giving away some random projects as failures.

Innovations and rewards

Should we reward someone for generating good ideas? I would be careful with this. I shared my point of view on the financial rewards in the "Reward scorecard" in the Examples chapter. And I believe that immediate financial motivation in this case won't drive any good behavior. Focus on the non-financial ways to award the person. At least recognize his or her contribution to the idea.

Step 8. When a measurement system stops working

The measurement system is supposed to help your organization by supporting business decisions and tracking your progress towards the goals, but in some cases we see the opposite. The indicators look good, but for some reason you earn less money; the customer satisfaction index is reported is in the green zone, but for some reason less clients extend their subscription. It looks like something is wrong with your performance measurement system.

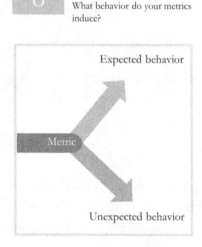

IMPACT
What behavior do your metrics induce?

Expected behavior

Metric

Unexpected behavior

According to my experience, there are two possible reasons for the problem in this case:

1. The gap between the business as it was modeled by the measurement system and the real business
2. Your employees found ways to game the measurement system.

In this chapter, we will discuss the possible reasons and the prevention plan.

How to detect the gap between a measurement system and real business

Performance measurement system is a digitalized model of your business. But sometimes people start thinking that the business mode is equal to the business. In one of the stories about Sherlock Holmes the dog did not bark and that led Holmes to the conclusion that the evildoer was recognized by the dog. For most people a barking dog means that something is wrong, but a silent dog doesn't arouse any suspicions. How does it matter in the business context? If you expect some indicator to increase its value, but it stays still, this might be for two reasons:

- The problem with the measurement system (the indicator that we've chosen was not the best ones)
- The problem with our understanding of the subject of measurement, the problem with the model that we have in mind

My recommendation is to look for something unexpected and analyze it in detail. Normally, we are good in analyzing the unexpected when something negative happens. For example, conversion rate was good, but no one bought the product. Train your team to detect the unexpected when something positive happens – the conversion rate was good, but the number of sales was two times more than you expected. Don't just credit this to luck, the problem might be deeper - with your understanding of the subject of measurement and the way you measure it.

Fighting piracy or killing marketing potential?

Let me share another example, it is about BSC Designer software. As a vendor of the software we understand that piracy is a problem. But in some markets a strange thing happens – illegal copies of the software among single users starts working as a powerful marketing tool for corporate users. It sounds like a paradox, but a classical approach to fighting piracy in that region could lead to a decrease in corporate sales in the long-term. In this case the problem was not in our measurement system (that included piracy-related indicators), but in our understanding of the market.

Quality control and validation of the data

Our software is localized to many languages and one of the challenges when you need to find a good translator is to understand who is doing a translation manually, who is using supportive tools like Translation Memory and who is simply copying the text to Google Translate. The simplest way to validate the translation results, is to show them to a native speaker, but there is also a technical way to do this.

We can look at the percent of minor errors that we can detect without knowing the language. For example, in the original strings we used parameters marked by "%s" or there might be a certain formatting style like for example using spaces before ":" sign. For example the line "%s, here are your results : " should be translated in Spanish as "%s, aquí tiene sus resultados : "

We are looking at how the "%s" and " : " markers were translated and can make some conclusions about the translation technique used without even knowing the language. For example, if you put the English line in Google Translate, the resulting Spanish translation will be: "% S, aquí están sus resultados:" While the Spanish translation is acceptable, the two markers indicate that it was not a manual translation - "S" symbol is uppercase, there is a space between % and "S" and there is no space before ":" In this way one can quickly find the machine translation.

That approach is good for filtering out the worst translation services, but there are some that will do a better job and search-and-replace the mentioned markers with the correct ones. Can we detect these cases without a deeper analysis by a native speaker? Look at the "silent dog" indicator, in this case the number of errors is one of them. If the translation is perfect and there is no single formatting error, then something is wrong. Try your best translators using that approach and you will be able to detect a certain error level, a small one, but detectable. If everything is perfect, then probably you just have not found the problem yet.

Conclusion

Make sure you train your team to look for the "silent dogs" as well. In our case we compared piracy indicators with the sales data, and the misaligned data made us research the subject of measurement and change our perception of the business environment. Look for the unexpected, its negative cases, and especially the positive ones.

Induced behavior

One of the most typical problems with performance measurement system (see the "Typical problems" chapter) is when employees start gaming the system. The game is to keep the performance indicators in the green zone, receive possible incentives, while not doing the real work properly.

If you think that I'm exaggerating, have a look at the Wells Fargo case[15] that was in the headlines in September 2016. The KPI-incentive system was in place, but instead of motivating employees to find the best ways to engage with the clients, it induced an unexpected behavior and pushed 5,300 employees towards gaming the system.

You might find a call center where employees are calling each other just to keep their "Number of calls" indicator in the green zone, or a web marketing specialist who drives traffic to a website without caring much about its quality. In the Soviet Union, one of the metrics to measure the effectiveness of the railway system was "ton/kilometer." And the simplest way to keep this indicator in the green zone was to move shipping containers across the country without any specific need.

Good news: it is possible to build a management system based on KPIs and avoid such problems. In the previous chapter, we discussed the steps to detect such cases, now let's talk about the ways to fix and prevent future problems.

Compare expected behavior and actual behavior

Do a quick test with your indicators. Take some metrics that were used for a month or two and try to answer these two questions:

---

[15] "Wells Fargo Fined $185 Million for Fraudulently Opening Accounts," Michael Corkery, 2016, The New York Times.

- What behavior did you *want to* induce with these indicators?
- What behavior did your indicators *actually* induce?

The second question is not that easy to answer. Be honest with yourself; don´t try to rely on your intuition, try to find the facts that support your guesses. My recommendation is to plan and do such checks regularly.

Example: fast food restaurant

Here is an example from a fast food business. Management of the restaurant noticed that they throw away too much food. They decided to change the situation and introduced some indicators for food waste. What behavior did they expect? The decrease in food waste of course! What actually happened? To reduce food waste employees stopped cooking a few hours before closing time. The fast food restaurant was not able to serve their clients a few hours before closing time!

Use a pair of "performance" and "quality" indicator

What might be a solution to the restaurant case? The solution is quite trivial, instead of using just one indicator, use a pair of indicators. One to confirm that the desired goal was achieved, another to track the quality aspect. In the case of a fast food restaurant the pair could be: "Food waste" (performance indicator) and "Menu options availability" (quality indicator).

In the case of Wells Fargo when employees were opening fake bank accounts, the pair could be "New accounts opened" (performance indicator) vs. "cashflow in new accounts within 3 months" (quality indicator). The idea is to back up the main indicator with a quality one.

Involve your team

In the fast food restaurant case behind the suggested KPIs there were the ideas dictated by the top managers. They saw the problem, and they decided to find a solution for it. In fact, it was more of a patch in its nature than a solution. Did they analyze why the food is wasted, did they analyze the possible ways to minimize it, did they ask their employees about it? Probably not, the KPIs were mandated top to bottom without any specific strategy in mind.

A better approach would be to involve the team. To do this I recommend following the format of Socratic dialogs. Instead of giving orders - ask questions. How can we minimize food waste? What difficulties might we face if we do this? What additional tools would you need? How would your job change? If the managers have the necessary skills of reading between the lines, they will be able to detect the possible execution problems in the early stages.

Simplify measurement system

In Barcelona, if you buy online a lot, like I do, you might notice a problem with delivery services. Sometimes truck drivers who are supposed to bring your purchase to your door report a fake "Failed delivery." It's not hard to imagine why this happens: managers are pushing truck drivers towards higher success delivery rates, sometimes it is not possible due to a high load, and sometimes truck drivers are not that willing to work before the weekend…

If we think about this problem we could probably come up with some technical solutions. For example, some courier services ask drivers to take a picture of the client's door that would confirm that they were there at a specified time; some use GPS trackers. But in many cases we don't need to invest in expensive logistics tools – just give your client an easy to use way to send you a feedback. You won't have a precise number of fake deliveries, but it is not required, sometimes, it's enough to get an idea about the trend.

Crash test your measurement system

Do this exercise with your teams. When your performance measurement system is ready, divide your team into the groups randomly. Ask one group to find the ways of possible misuse of the KPIs that you have. Ask another group to think about the protection plan. How would they change the KPIs, what additional metrics would they suggest? Make sure that everything is done is in a game format. I'm sure some interesting ideas for the improvement of performance measurement system will come up.

It's all about culture

If doing the root-cause analysis of the problems with the measurement system, you will soon find out that the actual reason is in a certain mindset of your employees.

- Even if you don't blame them for the failure, they might have a subconscious fear of this.
- Even if you gave them the freedom to choose any metrics they like, they will choose those that they found on the Internet.
- You might give them the best automation tools, but they won't update their scorecard regularly.

All of the mentioned behaviors are the signs that the performance measurement culture in your organization need to updated. In Step 9 of the KPI System I shared some specific recommendations to follow in this context.

Step 9. Decrease the cost and increase the value of measurement

When planning some measurement system we always have to think about the balance between the cost of the measurement and the value of the obtained results.

Medical doctors do this every day. Unless a patient is in an emergency situation, they don't start their examination with some invasive tests or a quite expensive tomographic scanning, instead they do some low cost measurements first, like measuring temperature and blood pressure.

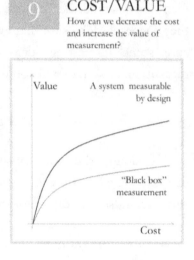

9 COST/VALUE
How can we decrease the cost and increase the value of measurement?

Repurpose the measurement

Before, we talked about a simple way to significantly decrease the cost of measurement. Do you remember the case of ROI measurement? Measuring dollar value of the *return* part implies high measurement cost, but if we agree that we just want to understand which of two methods created a higher value for the clients, then we can find the ROI data much easier.

Another example of a quick measure that decreases the cost of measurement significantly is *time*, a typical activity metric. Let's say there is a problem with the performance of new employees. We can start by a detailed and costly analysis, but I would recommend starting with a quick question – "How much time did each employee spend on the training?" 1 hour? 15 hours? The answer won't shed light on the details of training effectiveness, but it will give us a quick estimation of what we need. If most of the employees completed only a 1 hour training session, then the problem is obvious - they need to be trained more! If most of the new staff completed a 15 hour training, but still there is some kind of performance problem, then we can assume that the training needs to be improved, and we could consider investing in a sophisticated measurement system.

Definition of the expected precision

Another approach to the cost optimization is to be more specific about the precision of the results that we need. Let's say we need to measure the impact of an email marketing campaign for the product with average decision-purchase time equal to 6 months.

If we want to have high-precision results, then we would need to wait at least 1 year after the campaign. In many cases the person who received email is not the one who decides about the purchase, and the one who decides may not necessary sign the check. It means that we would need to do a personal survey with the customers to find out how they learned about the product. Not everyone will have time to participate in the survey, so we'd have to think about some additional motivation for the participants of the survey. I guess now you have a sense of what the cost of such measurement could be.

A simpler approach is to agree about a less precise measure. We understand that we won't be able to track all of the results, but just some part of them. Instead of waiting for 1 year, we wait for 6 months and analyze only the data that is in the CRM system. Yes, we know that it's not precise, but we are getting quicker results at a lower cost.

Combine repurpose and precision

Can we do an even less expensive and faster estimation? Let's redefine the purpose of measurement, and decrease precision even more. Instead of looking at a 6 month period, we can define some engagement metric together with the conversion rate for them, and then look at a shorter period. For example, we might know that those who downloaded the official case study are converted with 3% probability into being clients. Now, instead of waiting 6 months, we can have some quick results within a week. Besides optimizing the cost of measurement, we also optimized the time horizon. Now, if something is wrong with that email marketing campaign, we can correct it in the early stages.

Make system measurable "by design"

There is one approach to measurement that can decrease the cost and increase the value of measurement significantly. I call it "Measurable by design." Instead of trying to measure something afterwards, try to change your system beforehand, implement some additional measurement in it; and make it measurable by design.

Example: tradeshow

One of the cases that I suggest for the participants of the workshops is to imagine that they plan to attend a tradeshow with their product or service. My question is: how are you going to measure the results of your participation in the tradeshow afterwards?

The most typical answers normally are:

- We will collect business cards, input the data into our CRM system and will try to link future sales to the initial tradeshow leads
- We will give away some coupons and we'll use those coupons later to track the effectiveness of the event for our business
- Measure the effectiveness only in the sense of brand awareness

Example: discount coupon

Let´s take a discount coupon as an example. From the marketing viewpoint the coupon is supposed to increase the number of returning clients, and it is also the simplest mechanism to track cross marketing efforts. You might give out discount coupons on some promo event and later, when real customers will be using it, you will learn what promo event worked for you and what was ROI. Still, we cannot rely on the coupons in many cases:

- When the product is in a premium sector and the discount coupon will decrease its perceived value
- When the purchase cycle is long and different decision makers are involved

Example: tracking data with CRM

Another typical suggestion is to get all leads into the CRM system and use it to track the effectiveness. No matter how sophisticated your CRM system is, there is still a high probability that you won't be able to track back the sale to the original lead. One of the reasons is overlap of the marketing channels. Companies normally use different marketing tools and it will be hard to isolate the results of one channel from the results of another channel.

Brand awareness measure

Another popular solution to the tradeshow challenge is to replace real effectiveness measurement by the reputation metrics, for example measure the improvement of brand awareness. It might be a good way to approach the problem in this way, especially if you have a reliable brand metric. With social media analysis it is easier to get data for brand awareness metric, but the area of application will be limited to large consumers markets only.

Example: engage visitors with self-assessments

How would we need to change our business systems in order to reduce measurement efforts, and make measurement of the effectiveness more tangible? Getting back to the tradeshow example. What if you find a way to engage with your client more. What idea can you sell to your clients right at the tradeshow? If your product is in the cloud, then you can open a free test account for those who have an interest and make a short demo of what you have.

Another option that will work for any business is to suggest to the visitors of your booth to try some interactive self-assessment. Formulate the questions of self-assessment around the problems that people might face and the problems that your company can solve. Automate the assessment process with some iPad devices. People can answer a few questions about the current state of their business and get a short recommendation about the ways for the improvement. Your costs won't increase much, and you will have not just a contact, but a hot lead for your sales team. They will have a prospective client to work with, and they will have a starting base (client's problem as formulated in the self-assessment) for focusing the sales pitch. A side effect is that the leads will be more trackable in this case! That's how "measurable by design" approach works!

Can we do even better? How about redefining the purpose of measurement from the measuring "deals closed" to measuring "qualified leads?" Using the data from self-assessment surveys you can easily find out the number of the good leads that we have in just a few days not months after the tradeshow.

Example: this book is measurable by design

By the way, this book is also measurable by design. To get an idea of how it worked out for my readers I've implemented some instruments inside. In the "Downloads" section you will find links to some useful materials, like for example, a link to a print-friendly KPI System template in PDF format. The link goes to a special page on bscdesigner.com that won't be seen from a website and won't be indexed by the search engines. The web analytics data for this page will show the BSC Designer team if the book engages readers and their colleagues. A simple, yet still effective engagement measurement mechanism.

KPIs Housekeeping

The number of the performance indicators and their health status also influence the cost and value of measurement.

The right number of metrics

Overloading with KPIs is reported as one of the biggest challenge in the context of performance measurement. How can you avoid this? First of all, pass all of the metrics that you use throughout the steps of this KPI System. Remove those that are not aligned with your business strategy.

What is a perfect number of performance indicators? Performance metrics exist to support your business goals. To answer this question, you need to find out the number of the goals on your strategy map. In the best case scenario for each goal you will have at least one leading and one lagging indicator. This gives us a simple formula: Number of KPIs $\approx$ Number of goals * 2

What if you have much more metrics on your scorecard? In this case I would say that you have a scorecard for operation purposes, not a strategic one. Still, make sure that behind each metric on your scorecard there is some business context.

Indicators' update schedule

How often should we update the data for our KPIs? Is there any recommended schedule? There are several common-sense recommendations in this context.

- Update your indicators regularly when the benefit of the measurement is more than a cost of measurement

- If the cost of measurement is significant, update your indicators when you need data to support a new decision

A typical reporting period is between 1-4 weeks for operational indicators, and 2-6 months for strategic ones. For sure, there are a lot of exceptions: some process metrics are updated in real time and some metrics are updated for the annual reports only.

Recycle your indicators

Indicators appear on the scorecards because we are looking for the measurement system that would help to track the progress towards the goals, and validate achieved results. If the goal was 100% achieved or it was reinvented, then we probably don't need to be so active in the measurement of the indicators aligned with that goal. When the business context changes, the measurement system should be changed as well. What can we do with now useless metrics? Check out the decision matrix described in Step 6. If a metric still has a value for operations, move it to a respective dashboard, if the context has changed dramatically, just remove it from your scorecard.

Performance measurement culture

One of the ways to significantly improve your chances for success with measurement efforts, is to change the performance measurement culture in your organization. To keep it simple, let's think about culture as about a set of *behavior patterns*. What behaviors should we cultivate in the company, and what should be avoided? Below I share some insights on this topic.

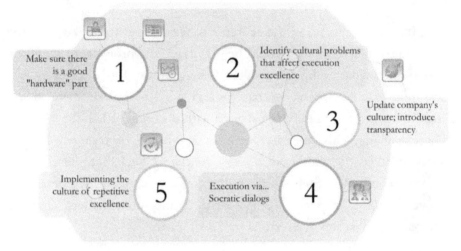

Figure 12 5 steps to make strategy scorecard more agile

Behavior patterns to cultivate

- Agreement on the terminology (goals, objectives, metrics, measures, indicators, targets, KPIs)
- Finding best indicators during the discussions with your team
- Using measurements to bring your team on the same page
- Seeing indicators in the red zone as opportunities to improve
- Using professional tools for the scorecards

Behavior patterns to avoid

- Mandating KPIs top to bottom
- Blaming someone for the KPIs that are in the red zone
- Using carrot-and-stick motivation style based on KPIs
- Using Excel for complex scorecard projects

In one of my articles[16] I shared a 5-step algorithm that one can follow to change measurement culture in their company. These steps are:

1. Find what needs to be broken: understand and work with existing behavior patterns
2. Focus on the challenging situations like indicators in the red zone, or the cases when it's hard to find good metrics
3. Tell stories about interesting performance measurement cases of course
4. Document it. A short 1-2 page instruction about KPIs is what your team needs.
5. Lead by example – in the case of performance measure it means that management should use performance metrics and be comfortable about discussing them with their team

Does quantified-self lead to the quantified company?

A movement called "quantified-self" promotes the need to regular collect data that might have an influence on our life – collectable indicators of the environment and various life-style indicators. With the development of the technologies the data collection might be easily merged with gamification and big data, thus producing some interesting insights.

---

[16] 5 Steps to Establish a Good Performance Measurement Culture, Aleksey Savkin, 2016, BSC Designer, http://www.bscdesigner.com/measurement-culture.htm

The topic of quantified-self movement is out of the scope of this book, but one side effect of this movement is of particular interest for me. People involved in the movement change their habits about how the data is collected and processed. The main shift is that *they* are willing to collect and process performance data. Compare this to the procrastination that managers see when it is time to compile a performance report for a company. I believe these experiments in personal life can be useful in a business context, especially as a way of establishing a good performance measurement culture.

Performance Measurement and Motivation

As reported in many surveys one of the problems related to the KPIs and performance measurement is a problem of motivation. People that might be enthusiastic about tracking the performance in the beginning, might lose this motivation very quickly. What's the trick to keeping teams motivated in terms of using performance measurement? I have two long-term hobbies – swimming and learning foreign languages, and in this chapter I'd like to share some of my findings in the context of motivation.

Swimming: the importance of intrinsic motivation

Some of my friends were doing swimming professionally. They joined local swimming clubs, and found a trainer who pushed the team towards better results. My approach was different – I valued the joy of the process more than the performance results, and saw the ultimate goal as having fun and staying healthy. It is good to know that it is one of the sports that you can practice life-long.

With time passing by, I've noticed one interesting thing: most of those who did swimming professionally in the beginning quit the sport. It looks like they were motivated more by their trainer and friends than by the process itself. On the contrary, my motivation is still with me.

Don´t take me wrong, I admire professional athletes, and recognize the need for the coach, I improved my swimming techniques significantly thanks to Michael Phelps's videos on YouTube and a few occasional classes with a professional trainer. My guess is that the key of long-term commitment is to recognize where the motivation is coming from. A good trainer would not push and motivate the team himself, instead he would spend time on developing intrinsic motivation.

The best thing about motivational aspect of KPIs that you can do is to recognize those motivated individuals (see the Quantified-self chapter), support their natural passion for understanding the nature of the things and give them the right tools. That's the reason why I used Saint-Exupéry's quote as an epigraph for the KPI System. It´s all about teaching your team to love the performance measurement itself.

Learning foreign languages: tailor made for your needs

As you can deduce from my name I'm a Russian native speaker, after graduating the university, I moved to Prague, Czech Republic and later in Barcelona, Spain. Learning Czech, some German and Spanish was something that you do naturally if you want to feel comfortable in both your professional and personal life. My first foreign language was English, and I did it in a more traditional way – group classes, individual classes, and text books. But I felt the real improvement when I had to actually use it to communicate with partners in the conferences and with some clients. When applied to a specific business domain, the language was very different from what I was learning in the textbooks.

For the next languages, under the pressure of time limits, I had to optimize. First I tried to compare group and individual classes. According to my calculations, individual classes were much more profitable in terms of time and money spend versus value obtained. I was able to engage more actively in the program of teaching, and after learning some basics. I switched to the cases that I believe are important in the first place for me. Instead of learning all the names for the rare animals that I hardly know in my native languages, I was more interested in the lexicon related to topics like real estate, travelling, and business. I structured the classes myself and my teachers were happy to help me with the nuances that were difficult. I was not following a text book written by some expert, I was writing my own textbook according to my needs, and it was a huge shift in the motivation.

How can this experience be applied to the domain of performance measurement? When you mandate KPIs, or when someone from your team finds KPIs on the Internet it's similar to learning by a textbook written by someone else. It looks professional, but it is far from being tailor-made for you. That's probably the reason why many people stop using foreign languages, and why many business say that the KPIs don't work for them. The solution is simple – start from scratch and build a measurement system that is right for your business.

Step 10. Build a scorecard

In the previous steps of the KPI System we have discussed the best practices that would help to find tailor-made performance indicators for your organization. What can you do with these indicators next? Build a scorecard! In this chapter I will share some advice on this topic.

Map your goals

In the first step of the KPI System I underlined the need to define the business context for any measurement system. How can we describe this context? One of the best approaches is to build a strategy map. In the contrast from a simple list of the goals, on the map we have an opportunity to explain how the goals are connected to each other. We can show the cause-and-effect logic between different goals.[17] This discipline is called strategy description, and is included in a wider discipline of strategy execution.

One of the most popular frameworks for strategy execution is the Balanced Scorecard. Following the Balanced Scorecard approach the goals should be grouped into these four perspectives:

- Financial perspective
- Client perspective
- Internal processes perspective
- Learning and growth perspective

---

[17] Strategy Maps: A Guide for Getting Started, Aleksey Savkin, 2014, BSC Designer, http://www.bscdesigner.com/strategy-maps-guide.htm

The goals from the different perspectives will be connected by the cause-and-effect links. From the strategy map it should be clear how the goals from Customer perspective are supporting the financial ones; and how the goals from Internal Perspective are supporting the goals from the Customer perspective.

In the first step of the KPI System we also discussed the need to have a list of stakeholders and breaking down the subject of measurement. This information is critical to the correct reading of the strategy map: write it down in the 2-3 pages of supporting documentation.

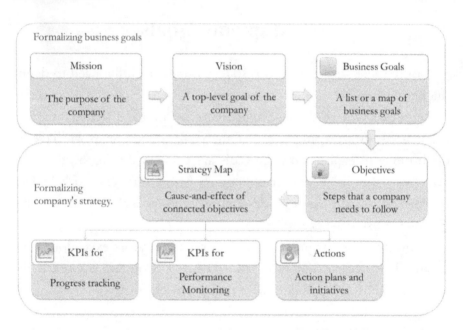

Figure 13 How goals, strategies, and KPIs are connected

Now with the strategy map we have a business context described. The next step would be to align performance metrics with those goals. Go ahead with the steps of the KPI System and find appropriate performance measures. Once found, you can visualize those indicators directly on the strategy map. The best option is to have at least 1 leading and 1 lagging indicator aligned with each of the goals. The next step would be adding more specific action plans or initiatives, and aligning them with the business goals on the strategy map. If built correctly, a strategy map is a powerful tool to support team discussions.

Align scorecards across the company

The practice of mapping important goals should not be limited to the top managers only. Ideally, in each business unit, there should be map of the goals and a performance scorecard. The main challenge in this case would be to align different scorecards between each other to give employees on all levels the sense of a coherent approach to the strategy.

A typical idea that top managers usually come up with is to *cascade* their scorecard to the lower levels by KPIs. This approach has two potential problems.

Avoid 100% top to down cascading

The term "cascading" itself might be misleading, as it implies a 100% top to bottom approach. In other words, line-level employees have no other choice, but to follow the direct orders dictated by the top managers. Their possible contribution to the strategy will be limited. A better approach would be to achieve a 40/60% mix where 40% of the goals are suggested by the top managers, and another 60% by the front-line employees. As for the choice of the term, a better option would be *alignment*.

Avoid cascading by indicators

Another problem is that the cascading is normally done by the indicators. What happens when one is trying to align two scorecards by the indicators? In many cases they fail to find a tangible link between indicators from the different levels. Let's say we have "Profit" indicator on the scorecard of a top manager. It might be successfully cascaded to the scorecard of the sales department, but how should it be cascaded to the scorecard of an HR specialist or any other department that is not involved in generating profit directly? Can we cascade a "profit" indicator down to the level of, let's say, a webmaster who is designing a new template for a corporate website? In other words, can we make a webmaster responsible for their part of the profit directly? Technically it is possible, but what kind of behavior will we drive in this way?

Example: Cascading by business goals

In one of my articles[18] I shared in the details my approach to cascading. A short recommendation would be to align/cascade a scorecard by business goals, not by indicators. First understand how the goals from one scorecard are supporting the goals from another; then if necessary, find the way to link them by the indicators.

Let's take a website redesign as an example. How do the goals on the front-level might support the goals on the level of top managers? In this case the goal chain might be like this one:

- Redesign a website > more user engagement > more qualified leads > increase in profit.

Or we can also track a different route:

- Resign a website > make the knowledge base more useable > less requests to the customer support > decrease in support costs > increase in profit

---

[18] Balanced Scorecard Cascading: Make Your Strategy Resonate with Company, Aleksey Savkin, 2014, BSC Designer, http://www.bscdesigner.com/cascading.htm

We showed how a goal from a lower business level is supporting a top-level goal. Now we can align these two goals by the indicators. The webmaster won't be responsible for the increase in profits directly, but he or she will need to make sure that the usability of the website increases. Respectively, on the level of the webmaster we will have a usability metrics. If we can define the business context well enough, we can even find a dollar equivalent for a usability metric.

Different approaches to the alignment

In practice the approach to alignment/cascading varies from company to company. In one of my articles[19] I categorized 12 typical cases of cascading. One of the most widely used approaches (not necessary the most efficient) are cases 4 and 8 from the above-mentioned article. Here are the diagrams for those cases:

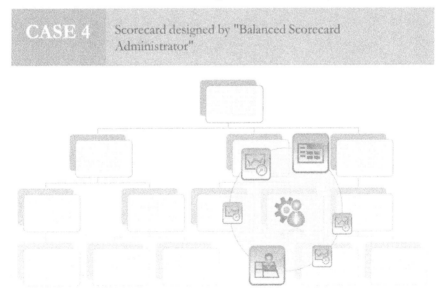

CASE 4   Scorecard designed by "Balanced Scorecard Administrator"

BSC Administrator does everything related to the scorecard. The strategy map might appear, but it is more about a map than about strategy.

---

[19] 12 Examples of How Companies Organize and Cascade Balanced Scorecards, Aleksey Savkin, BSC Designer, http://www.bscdesigner.com/bsc-cascading-examples.htm

CASE 8   Accountability bias

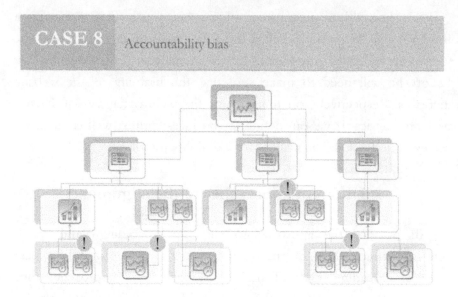

Companies that do too much of this KPI-powered "carrot and stick" model will soon find out that their employees are trying to game the system in some way.

What is a recommended approach? It depends on the company and its goals, in most cases the first thing that I'd recommend doing is to make sure that the insights for the goals and the KPIs are the product of a discussion rather than just mandated top to bottom:

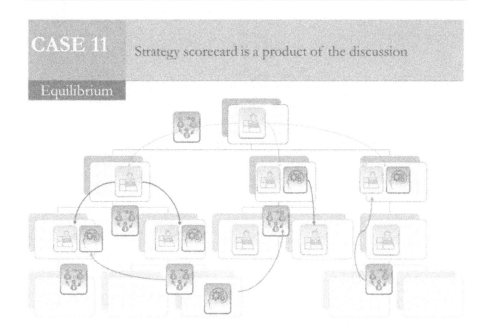

CASE 11 Strategy scorecard is a product of the discussion

Equilibrium

A role of the scorecard practitioner appears. Around 60% of ideas translated top to bottom and 40% were suggested by the line-level managers.

Here are some conclusions for this chapter:

- Involve all levels of the organization into the strategy discussion and execution
- Creating a scorecard and strategy map for each business unit
- Avoid the term "cascading," replace it with "alignment"
- Align the scorecards by business goals, not by KPIs

Using automation tools

If something will happen with KPI, will you be notified?

In one of the previous chapters we were talking about the balance between the cost of measurement and the value of measurement. One of the important cost factors are scorecard maintenance and reporting.

You are wasting your time when:

-   Fixing some broken formulas in spreadsheet software or trying to create multi-level scorecards there
-   Trying to draw some visually appearing strategy map in presentation software
-   Trying to fit goals, metrics, and initiatives on one page to make the report look nice

Presentation and spreadsheet software are good in the prototype stage, but when your scale is bigger you need to choose a professional tool.

AUTOMATION
Will you be notified if
something happens?

BSC DESIGNER
www.bscdesigner.com

SET UP KPIS | CALCULATE
PERFORMANCE | TRACK OVER
TIMEFRAME | DASHBOARDS |
STRATEGY MAPS | ALERTS

Alternatives to Excel

Professional scorecard software doesn't necessary imply any investment costs. Many software vendors have a freeware versions of their tools with some basic functionality. Probably you won't find all of the fancy reports there, but the basic scorecard math will be there. For example, at BSC Designer we have a BSC Designer Light – a freeware version of BSC Designer. It has some basic features for the KPIs and it is sufficient for getting started with a performance measurement project. The scorecards created in that version can later be used in the PRO and cloud-based versions.

What functions to look for

Among the software packages for the KPIs there are many tools that allow drawing nice dashboards. My recommendation is to find one that will help to describe and visualize your business context as well. From the functional point of view dashboards give us a nice picture of how the company is doing now, but they provide very limited information about the business context. In contrast from a dashboard, a good strategy map helps to visualize the business goals, cause-and-effect connections between them, aligned leading and lagging indicators, and initiatives. Compare this dashboard and the strategy map below:

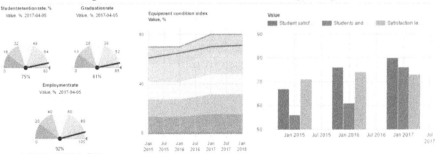

Figure 14 An example of a dashboard for university scorecard

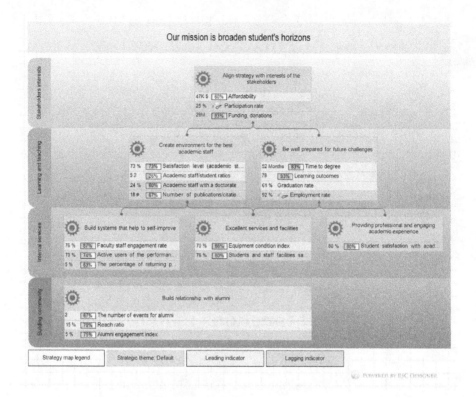

Figure 15 An example of a strategy map for university scorecard

Dashboards and strategy maps tell different stories, and in the case of the strategy map, I'd say that the story is more helpful for a team in terms of understanding the context and focusing their efforts.

My suggestion for any business professional who is looking for an automation tool is to find a software where at least you can have a list of your goals and align KPIs with them. The best approach would be a possibility to visualize your goals, metrics, and initiatives directly on the strategy map. BSC Designer and some of its direct competitors can do this, so you have options to choose from.

It's a team game

I hope I have expressed this idea clearly in the previous chapters: indicators work much better if they are the product of a discussion. The real value of the KPIs is not in the fact of just having them, but of the processes of finding and using them together with your team. When shortlisting a scorecard software, find a cloud-based one, as that will make collaboration between members of your team easier.

Give a try to BSC Designer Online

I invite you to try both cloud-based BSC Designer Online (www.webbsc.com) and BSC Designer PRO for Windows OS (www.bscdesigner.com). There are two important reasons to do this: you can try both products for free, and there are some good templates of the KPI and business scorecards available for free download. For more information see the details in the Examples and Downloads chapters.

Conclusion

When you are working on a prototype of your scorecard, you can easily do it without any software or using Excel spreadsheets, but when the goal is to build a KPI or Strategy Scorecard, the use of automation tools is highly recommended.

In the next chapter, we will discuss how to get all your KPIs together and build a scorecard. I would recommend going in that direction only with a proven automation tool employed.

Examples

It's easier to start with a performance measurement system when you have some examples in front of your eyes. Some of the examples discussed in this chapter include specific metrics, some include just general directions to follow. That was done on purpose, as I'm not trying to give you ready-to-use metrics to implement, instead I'm trying to teach you to create your own strategies.

Beyond standard financial KPIs

In this chapter I'm not going to talk about EBITDA and other financial metrics that are promoted as "must have" for any scorecard. Instead, I'd like to focus on several conceptual directions that one needs to think about. They were discussed in various parts of the book, and it makes sense to summarize them here.

- **Value metric.** This metric is to emphasis that the business of any organization is about creation of the value for their clients. Do you know how your clients perceive the value that you create? Here is a tip: it's not about mapping all of the services that you have, and all features that you have in the product.
- **Quality metric.** The high perceived quality of your product or service leads to the company's success in the long-term. Make sure that it is the market and customers who decide about the quality, not your marketing team.
- **What is accumulated.** Not a typical metric, I've discussed it in Step 7 of the KPI System. What is accumulated in your business? Subscriptions, customer data base, relationship with the clients, IP? Do you own these legally? Do you know how

this accumulated value changes over time? Your efforts to find this metric are even more valuable than the metric itself.

- **Systems and their mechanics.** The bottom line of any organization are the business systems that work for you. Make sure you know how these systems are working. Look at the conversion rates, what was happening during peak loads, and where the main costs and profits are accumulated. A good visual picture like these here will help:

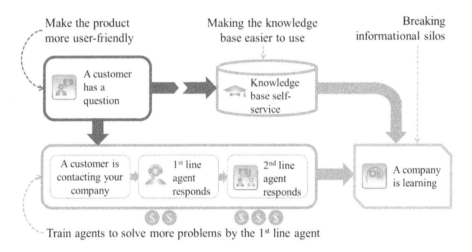

Figure 16 A customer service model: processes, costs, response plan

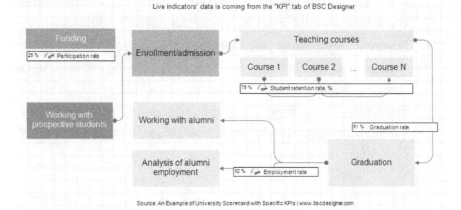

Figure 17 An example of the main processes in an university

- **Broken appointments.** If you consider time to be one of your most valuable resources, make sure you track the cost of broken appointments, and implement a plan to reduce them.
- **Customer metrics.** Know your customer. Know how much it costs to get a new one, how long does a customer stay with you, and what is the customer's lifetime value.
- **Customer touch points.** Any business is about working with customers. Customer give us a valuable feedback, they vote for certain functions of the product with their money, they compare us with the competitors, and decide on the value for their money. If you have more high quality "touch points" with your customers, you can expect better results. Everything counts – calls to the customer service, marketing materials on your website, newsletters, customers' experience when they purchase your service, or stop using it. The starting point would be to map all those touch points and understand how the value is created there.
- **Silver bullet metric.** A good task for a workshop format. The participants discuss various candidates for the metrics, talk about

different types of indicators, and then I ask them to choose just one indicator that will be the most valuable for their business. This indicator is normally a *leading one* and *strategic* (focused on the change). If you could have one single indicator on your dashboard, what would it be?

In the chapters below I share more examples of the KPI scorecards. You will find there some specific metrics, but the true value of these examples is in the methods used for working with the indicators. When applying it to your domain, focus on those methods, not just on the KPIs.

Training scorecard: 4-level measurement model

Let's start with a case when we deal with time lagging, and multidimensional performance results. A typical training is an example of such a situation. On the one hand, the effectiveness of a training is lagging in time and cannot be measured right away after the training: we need to give the trainees some time to implement what they have learnt and only then can the real performance improvement be analyzed.

On the other hand, if we ask a person who is leaving a training room "How was the training?" we will have some immediate answer, and if start thinking about the reasons for such an answer, we will be able to define at least several dimensions that the student based his or her opinion on. For example, the training might look great because of the very engaging presentation style that the lector used, or on the contrary, the materials of the training might be excellent, but the speaker was not able to capture the attention of an audience.

Back in 1954 Donald Kirkpatrick suggested a 'four level' model for training course evaluation that suggests looking at the training from these four perspectives: Reaction, Learning, Behavior, and Impact. If applied to the training domain we should focus our measurement efforts on the immediate after-training feedback, quantify learnings (via tests for example), understand if/how those learnings were applied in practice, and finally if/how those practical applications helped to improve the ultimate business performance.

From my point of view, the most challenging task in the context of training evaluation is to understand if the resources of the company were spent on infotainment-style training (that normally get high scores in "Reaction" stage), or on the performance-shifting training with the highest score in the "Behavior" and "Impact" stage. When I share this thought in front of a group of people, someone normally argues: what's the benefit of analyzing past results? I'd say it depends on the approach of the company to the training process.

If the approach is more like testing a hypothesis that some training is useful, then probably a company, won't do training for the whole organization, but for a control group of individuals first. For sure, we should remember about the uncertainty principle described in the "Experiments" chapter.

In one of my articles I have discussed in detail how to build a scorecard for training[20], what I wanted to point out in this book is that this multi-level approach can be applied to many domains. For example, we will see a similar approach in the marketing scorecard example below.

Effectiveness of the leadership training

I've got this curve ball from one of our clients: "How can we measure the effectiveness of the leadership training?" he asked. We started a discussion, and the first problem that we faced was the absence of the agreement about what *leadership* is. We even could not agree if Napoleon was a good leader, or if he was just the person who ordered solders to open a fire against civilians. To put the discussion on a more productive path, I shared a story about Alexander the Great refusing fresh water once while passing the Gedrosian desert with his army, as it was written by Greek author Arrian of Nicomedia[21]. That action inspired not just the army that Alexander was leading, but many future generations of leaders. Although we have not agreed on the specific definition of leadership, we have agreed on certain behavior patterns that a good leader might have as applied to the domain of the client.

---

[20] Training Scorecard: From Exam Scores to KPI Effectiveness, Aleksey Savkin, BSC Designer, http://www.bscdesigner.com/training-scorecard.htm

[21] Alexander in the Bactrian desert, Livius, 2002, http://www.livius.org/sources/content/curtius-rufus/alexander-in-the-bactrian-desert/

My next question was about the expectations of the client from that leadership training. I asked: "Why did you decide to send your managers to that leadership training?" The idea was that the managers would learn some new skills and apply them in their daily job, and the expectation was that the team will be more motivated and engaged. After some discussion we were able to narrow down the profile of a motivated and engaged person. One employee who was working in the company looked like an ideal of motivation and engagement. When someone mentioned a minor problem, she took some notes and in a few days she sent a follow-up email with some actionable ideas, there was no need to assign her a task, control the execution or whatever, the results were always great…

My last question was about the purpose of measurement. I asked: "Why do you want to know the effectiveness of the leadership training?" From the client's respond, I learnt that the idea was to understand if it is working on a small scale, and if it makes sense to involve other managers.

What was the verdict? We had no agreement on what leadership is, but we agreed that the evaluation horizon for the leadership skills is long-term in its nature. Instead of waiting years to validate the results, we can probably track more tangible effects of the training. Using the four level model the result would look like:

- **Impact**. The ultimate goal was to increase motivation, so in the long-term we could count the percent of highly motivated and engaged individuals (compared to the ideal employee described above).
- **Behavior**. Taking a step backward, there should be some actions that are supposed to increase the motivation.
- **Learning**. One more step backward: what's preceding those actions? The long list of potential ideas that leaders are supposed to test.

- **Reaction**. Was the leadership training good enough to inspire managers who passed it?

We agreed on the assumption that managers who pass the leadership training will learn some new ideas. Five ideas out of 10 will result into an action, and one action out of 5 actionable ideas will generate a tangible improvement in motivation that a company will be able to quantify compared to the profile of an ideal employee that they had.

A quick estimation of the effectiveness of leadership training would be to look at the list of ideas; a better estimation would be to look at the ideas implemented (actions), finally the best estimation would be to look at the performance outcomes of those actions.

Marketing scorecard: conversion funnel model

An example of marketing scorecard teaches us a very simple, but still powerful idea: for any business system there are conversion rates that we can easily measure and change.

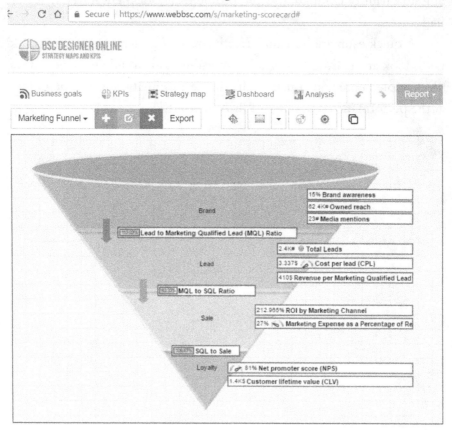

Figure 18 An example of the marketing funnel with live indicators

Let's build a sample marketing funnel: Brand -> Lead -> Sale -> Loyalty. For each level, we can define a conversion rate:

- Lead to marketing qualified leads, %
- Marketing qualified leads to sales qualified leads, %
- Sales qualified lead to sales, %

On each level we can define additional performance metrics. What's the benefit of such a funnel model? It helps to see the cause-and-effect in numbers. Plan to increase sales by 15%? With a funnel model, you already have an action plan –increase the conversion rate for each level. For more marketing KPIs and a live example of a Marketing Scorecard, I'd suggest checking out the article: "Guide for Tracking Marketing KPIs and Measuring Profitability."[22] Below you will find a copy of a strategy map that we discussed in that article.

---

[22] Guide for Tracking Marketing KPIs and Measuring Profitability, Aleksey Savkin, 2015, BSC Designer, http://www.bscdesigner.com/marketing-kpis.htm

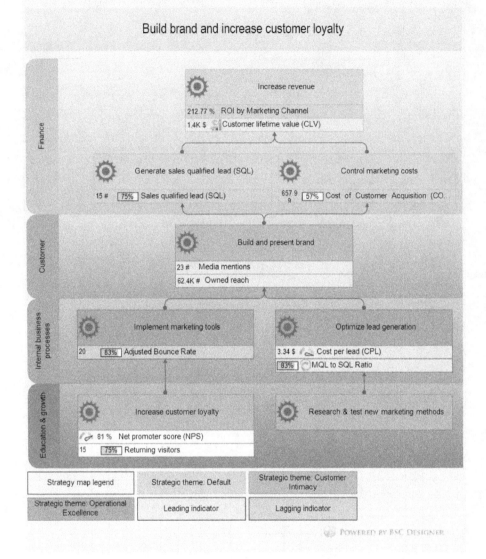

Figure 19 An example of strategy map for marketing department

Sales scorecard: the viewpoint of different stakeholders

Another example that I'd like to discuss is a scorecard for sales. In this example, I'd like to demonstrate an approach to the performance indicators that takes into account different stakeholders. In contrast from a simple list of KPIs, I suggest analyzing sales performance from the perspective of sales specialist, manager of sales department, and top manager. Each of these stakeholders will have their own interest in the sales measurement.

Layer 1. Operational level

On the operational level, we can present a sales process like how we did it for marketing, e.g. build a sales funnel. In this funnel we can track how the state of the client changes from "initial request" to "qualified leads" and then to "sale":

- Initial request
- Lead
- Meaningful conversation
- Qualified lead
- Sale

The indicators for Layer 1 might be the typical conversion rate indicators like:

- Reach Rate, %
- Pas Rate, %
- Conversion Rate, %

A direction for improvement would be to look at the sales process in more details and define metrics for the specific operational challenges that your sales team faces.

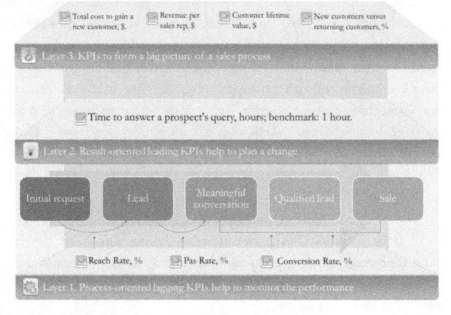

Figure 20 3 Layers of sales performance scorecard

Layer 2. Management level

On the next level, we are not that interested in the process metrics, but in the tangible results of a properly functioning sales system. Instead of analyzing the conversion rates like we did on Layer 1, we will focus on the metrics that are leading ones in the context of sales process, for example:

- Time to answer a prospect's query, hours; benchmark: 1 hour.

Layer 3. "Big picture" view

In this layer we are looking at the sales from the perspective of top manager, it is a "big picture" view. At this level we assume that the sales system is working properly. We have indicators from Layer 1 and Layer 2 to make sure that it is. The "big picture" view would focus on the sales process in general, we could focus on such metrics as:

- Total cost to gain a new customer, $.
- Revenue per sales rep, $
- Customer lifetime value, $
- New customers versus returning customers, %

The benefits of this approach

By following this approach we recognized that the sales process involves many stakeholders, and depending on the perspective we want to see, we can focus our measurement system. If you want to learn more details about this approach, I'd recommend reviewing the article "3 Layers of Sales KPIs Aligned With Business Strategy[23]" available on the BSC Designer website.

---

[23] 3 Layers of Sales KPIs Aligned With Business Strategy, Aleksey Savkin, 2014, BSC Designer, http://www.bscdesigner.com/3-layers-of-sales-kpis.htm

Reward scorecard: does it work?

I know that for most business professionals a scorecard is first of all a way to do performance evaluations and calculate various bonuses. But frankly, saying I do NOT recommend using KPI scorecards in this way, especially for the roles that are not related to sales directly.

Even for sales representatives, bonus metrics might be tricky. Imagine a situation when an employee who works in sales needs to choose between two options for the customer – one with higher value for customers, but a lower incentive to be paid; another with less value for the customer, but with a higher incentive to be paid. What would be the choice? It depends on the person for sure, but in a general case, by building such incentives into the system we are forcing employees to find a way to game the indicators. In the "Typical problems" chapter we have discussed some real-life examples that confirm that point of view.

Another question is what behavior does management want to drive by using a bonus system? Back in 1960, Douglas McGregor introduced[24] his XY Theory:

- The "Theory X" states that people by their nature hate the work and need to be managed by the "carrot and stick" style;
- The "Theory Y" states the opposite – it recognizes that people are motivated by self-esteem and creative tasks.

By active use of the bonus systems, managers shift a company's culture to the "Theory X" style management. All systems related to the talent management might be "infected" by this approach.

What would be a better approach? In the "Compensation and Reward KPI Best Practices"[25] article published on the BSC Designer, I

---

[24] Douglas McGregor, The Human Side of Enterprise, 1960, McGraw-Hill

analyzed 4 possible levels for the reward models used. Have a look at the diagram from that article to determine what level s your company is on.

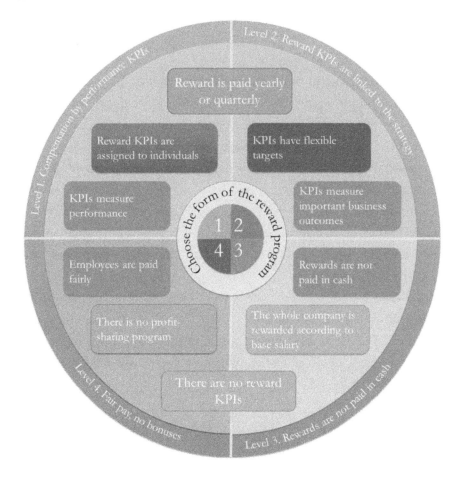

Figure 21 Compensation and reward KPI best practices. 4 level model.

The choice of the reward program depends on a specific business context and a company's background, in a general case I would recommend:

- Avoid cash incentives, and use them carefully for sales staff

---

[25] Compensation and Reward KPI Best Practices, Aleksey Savkin, 2013, BSC Designer
http://www.bscdesigner.com/reward-kpi-best-practices.htm

- Replace individual rewards with company-level rewards
- Pass reward metrics through the steps of the KPI System to make sure that there is a tangible purpose behind them
- Use a pair of performance and quality metrics (see Step 8 of the KPI System)

What about the bonuses for the top managers? In many cases the design of a bonus scorecard is when top managers decide on the best metrics to justify their bonuses. The paradox of such an incentive system is that in the case of negative performance, top managers are paid "just" salary, and in the case of positive performance they are paid salary + bonuses. A better alternative would be to replace bonuses in cash with bonuses in the form of stock options. Henry Mintzberg, author of Strategy Safari, shared in his article[26] in the Wall Street Journal an even more extreme opinion. He stated that "the problem is that they [executive bonuses] exist!"

Obviously, companies have to compete for the talents on the market, and a developed bonus system is an attractive benefit for the new hires. When you introduce a bonus system make sure you are have a plan to control its effect on the behavior patterns. We talked about this on the Step 8 of the KPI System.

---

[26] No More Executive Bonuses!, Henry Mintzberg, 2009, The Wall Street Journal

University scorecard: the use of ranking index

In March 2017 I was researching the best practices about creating a scorecard for educational organizations like colleges, universities, and schools. If you are an education professional, you can find the results in the published article[27].

One interesting finding is that many universities used data from rankings systems on their scorecards. In the educational domain, there are a lot of reputed rankings:

- QS Top Universities
- THE (THE World University Rankings), and
- ARWU (Academic Ranking of World Universities)

My recommendation for the business professionals is: even if you are not working in the education field, try finding organizations that do ranking for your business domain. Authors of the ranking system normally share the methods and indicators used to support their rankings. The found indicators will probably be too vague to be used for the performance management, but the methods used to obtain the data for these ranking might be very useful. Last but not least, you will have some proven data for the benchmarks.

---

[27] An Example of University Scorecard with Specific KPIs, Aleksey Savkin, 2017, BSC Designer, http://www.bscdesigner.com/university-scorecard.htm

When the problem is not in measurement

One of the challenges from our clients was to build a scorecard that would help them to measure customer service performance. After a short analysis, we found out that the main challenge is not the customer service itself, but the emergency nature of the problems that had to be resolved by the customer service. A root-cause analysis showed that most of those problems were emergencies only because clients were procrastinating and waiting until the last days before the deadline to solve them.

A standard approach to that problem would be to build a scorecard with classical indicators like waiting time, response efficiency, % of returning problems, etc., but that would not address the actual problem. Together with the client we came up with a strategy that would introduce certain changes in how they deal with the customers.

The new model was inspired by how auto dealers provide a technical service. Owners of the car understand the importance of changing oil regularly and doing other maintenance service. They accept paying for this service and are not waiting for the bigger problem to appear. We suggested for the client to try this approach. With that change in mind the performance scorecard was built differently. The measurement efforts of the customer were divided into 3 main directions:

1. Making sure that clients are involved in the maintenance program
2. Making sure that most of the typical problems are detected during that maintenance program
3. Making sure that the team is learning from the rest of the cases that were not systematized yet

This is another example that underlines the importance of the strategic approach to the performance measurement. In many cases instead of measuring something we need to understand what changes can be introduced into the system to make it serve the needs of the organization better.

More examples

If you are interested in finding more examples of KPIs in certain business contexts, I suggest for you to visit the Examples sections at www.bscdesigner.com:

- http://www.bscdesigner.com/real-bsc-examples.htm

At the time of writing this book we had 16 examples of the business scorecard. Each of the scorecards includes a list of sample business goals, KPIs, and a strategy map. All the scorecards are available in .BSC format that can be viewed online with cloud-based BSC Designer Online, or can be downloaded and viewed off-line with BSC Designer PRO or freeware BSC Designer Reader.

I suggest for the readers of the book to review those examples for some inspiration and specific ideas. If necessary, use them to start your own business scorecard project.

How to measure the value of this book

We have discussed many examples where the KPI System might be helpful. What about this book itself as a subject of measurement. Can we use the KPI System to analyze the value of this book? Let's give it a try! This exercise might be helpful for any business book, not just for this one.

Four-level model

I suggest using the Four Levels model (see the Training Scorecard example above) as a frame for the analysis. We can look at the book from the four perspectives and for each perspective formulate several questions that we can use later a base for quantification and measurement.

- **Reaction**. Was it easy to read? Were the examples engaging? Were the illustrations attractive? Does it feel like a good value for money?

- **Learning**. How many ideas have you highlighted with a yellow marker? How many ideas have you written down on the "Space for your ideas" page? How many insights have you shared in the talks with your colleagues?

- **Behavior**. Did you try the ideas from the book in practice? Did you use the checklists and templates from the book? How did your approach to the KPIs change?

- **Impact.** In the long-term, can you say that some of your business achievements can be credited back to the ideas learnt from the book?

All these questions can be quantified and converted into measurements if necessary.

Understanding dollar value

We can go even further: we can measure a dollar value of the information in any business book as perceived by a specific business professional. I know this is a very rough estimation, so all brilliant authors of business literature, please forgive me for such an approach, but the good thing is that it works:

- **Inputs**: book price in dollars plus dollar equivalent of your time spent on reading. Book price, $ + Hours spent on reading * Hour rate, $.
- **Outputs**: immediate insights after reading the book applicable to your business; insights converted into the specific actions and their estimated dollar value.
- **Expected results**: tangible business improvements that you credit back to the ideas from the book (the horizon can be 5 years or more); If needed, you can additionally quantify these improvements by their monetary value.

The purpose of measurement

Aren't we missing something? What about the purpose of the measurement! What if the purpose is to understand if that book was a good investment of time and money? In this case, with just one applicable insight learnt from the book we can give a positive answer. But this answer and the result of measurement would be lagging in time.

It is more interesting to align the measurement with some learning or change strategies. For example, to understand if it makes sense to follow up with other ideas of the author and if it makes sense to scale the ideas from the book to the rest of your organization.

Action plan

Another benefit of this measurement exercise is that it helps to understand how the business books can create the value. The highest value is not in the first impression, and even not in the long list of generated ideas, but in what was finally implemented. That's why for this book I encourage you not just to read the text, but to also choose some of the ideas that are resonating with what you are doing, and give them a try.

Thank you for your time! Feel free to share your achievements in the comments for this book on Amazon website where others can learn from them!

Appendix 1. 10 Steps KPI System Template Checklist

Find a link to the print-friendly version in the "Downloads" chapter.

1 MEASUREMENT PRISM
Define subject, purpose, and stakeholders

Break-down
subject of
measurement

Define the purpose
of measurement

Define
Stakeholders

What is the subject of measurement? What do you want to measure?

_____

Who are the stakeholders? Who has an interest?

1. _____ 2. _____

3. _____ 4. _____

Break-down the subject of measurement into tangible parts:

1. _____   2. _____

3. _____   4. _____

Why do we measure? How are we going to use the results of the measurement?

_____

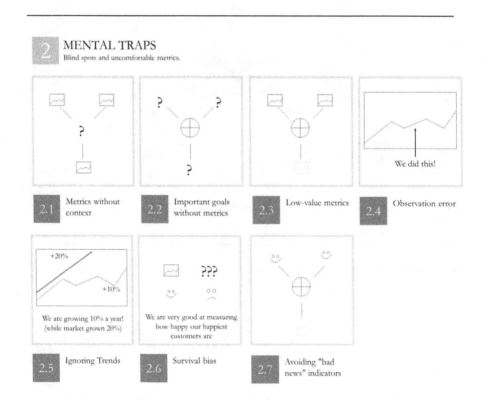

2 MENTAL TRAPS
Blind spots and uncomfortable metrics.

2.1 Metrics without context	2.2 Important goals without metrics	2.3 Low-value metrics	2.4 Observation error

We did this!

2.5 Ignoring Trends	2.6 Survival bias	2.7 Avoiding "bad news" indicators

We are growing 10% a year! (while market grown 20%)

We are very good at measuring how happy our happiest customers are

Checklist for the existing indicators:

- ☐ There are no metrics without context
- ☐ All important goals have metrics aligned with them
- ☐ There are no easy to measure, but low-value metrics
- ☐ We know about observation error and take it into account when analyzing the data
- ☐ We have benchmarks for our industry
- ☐ We adjusted measurement systems to learn from both - success and failures
- ☐ We have "bad news" indicators on our scorecards

3 BIRD'S-EYE LOOK
Constraints, Leading, and lagging indicators.

4 UNKNOWN
Is there something that you still cannot measure?

LEADING METRICS
Find success factors and distinguish them from other inputs.

OBSERVATION

Teach your team to read between the lines

Look for the absence of something

LAGGING METRICS
Distinguish results valuable for the stakeholders from all other outputs and activities.

BOTTLENECKS METRICS
What is limiting the value that you can create for the stakeholders?

CONTROLLED EXPERIMENTS
By experimenting we are interfering with the subject of the experiment

- ☐ We have mapped the analyzed system including its inputs and outputs

The success factors and leading indicators:

1. _____

2. _____

3. _____

Performance outcomes and lagging indicators:

1. _____

2. _____

3. _____

Constraints (what's limiting our system for 2x performance increase?):

1. _____

2. _____

3. _____

Are there still some challenging indicators? Here are the experiments/observations that we plan to get more information about them:

1. _____

2. _____

3. _____

5 METRIC SETUP
Scale, Formula, Weight.

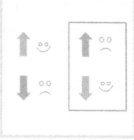

| 5.1 | Measurement scale | 5.2 | Optimization direction and performance | 5.3 | Weight of the indicator |

For each leading and lagging indicator the following details are defined in the automation software:

☐ Scale of measurement
☐ Optimization direction and performance formula
☐ Relative weight

6 SORTING METRICS
How do you prioritize indicators on your scorecard?

	URGENT	NOT URGENT
IMPORTANT	Operational goals and their metrics	Strategic goals and their metrics
NOT IMPORTANT	Something to outsource to the scorecard of other department	Why do you still have these goals and metrics on your scorecard?

We have both strategic (focused on change) and operational indicators (focused on the best practices), here is how we prioritize the measurement efforts:

	Urgent	Not Urgent
Important		
Not important		

FIND LEADING METRICS
How to find strategic (change) goals and metrics for them

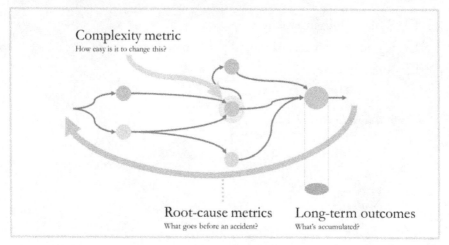

Complexity metric
How easy is it to change this?

Root-cause metrics   Long-term outcomes
What goes before an accident?   What's accumulated?

Use the checklist below to generate some insights for strategic and leading indicators:

- ☐ Do a root-cause analysis to find out what's preceding expected results
- ☐ Reducing complexity of the system might be a good strategic goal
- ☐ What outcomes are accumulated in the organization in the long-term?
- ☐ What is the value for the end-users?
- ☐ What is quality for the end users, how do they perceive it?

Impact checklist:

- ☐ We analyzed how the real behavior induced by the indicators is different from the expected one
- ☐ We have a pair of performance and quality indicators for the most important goals

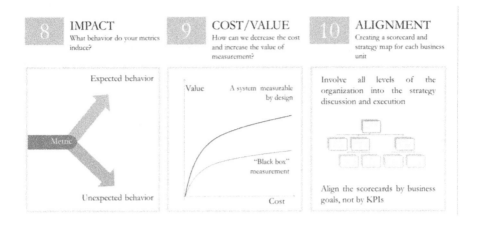

Cost and value of measurement:

☐ We know the error level of measurement

☐ We choose the measurement tools that are relevant for the desired precision

☐ Measurement is incorporated into our systems, they are "measurable by design"

Alignment

☐ The strategy scorecards are created for all key business units

☐ The scorecards from the different levels are aligned by business goals

☐ Some scorecards are connected by the indicators

Software automation:

☐ We stopped using spreadsheets after the prototype stage

☐ We created strategy maps to explain the context of measurement

☐ With our software tool, we can align goals with metrics and action plans

☐ We use multi-user software that supports teamwork

Download template: http://www.bscdesigner.com/10-step-kpi-system-download.htm

Appendix 2. Downloads

To make this book even more useful I provide the links to some downloads. Enjoy!

Examples

- Examples of the KPIs and Business Scorecards: http://www.bscdesigner.com/real-bsc-examples.htm

Software

- Cloud-based BSC Designer Online: www.webbsc.com
- Windows Desktop BSC Designer PRO: www.bscdesigner.com

Template

- Download the print-friendly version of the 10 Step KPI System: http://www.bscdesigner.com/10-step-kpi-system-download.htm

Speaking and workshops

I'll be happy to share my experience about performance measurement and strategy execution. My favorite format is a full-day hands-on workshop and the shorter keynote presentations.

If you feel like something needs to be adjusted in your performance measurement system, or you just need someone to see what's going on with fresh eyes, then I can probably add some value.

To discuss the details, please contact the BSC Designer team at www.bscdesigner.com

A Space for Your Ideas

CPSIA information can be obtained
at www.ICGtesting.com
Printed in the USA
BVHW032147110620
581388BV00001B/87

9 781365 900716